I0487087

Table of Contents

Author Ross R. Olney, who has written more than two hundred books because writing books is what he loves to do, (and especially books about sex and motor racing; he is an expert on the latter, and feels sure that very few are experts on the former). Here, in a leisure moment in a restaurant/bar on Olvera Street in Los Angeles, he enjoys relaxing.

Most of his books were published by major New York trade publishers, and are available everywhere, but books like this one give him far more content control, and are more fun to write since he can say what he wants to say and not what some New York editor says he should say. (Photo by Saylor Milton)

ISBN # 978-1-387-54904-7

FOR MODERN MEN ONLY

By Ross R. Olney

Chapter One

There is a joke going around today that in one way shows the power that women have over men, not that most men would spend a great deal of time arguing over a pretty well known truth like this. A quick glance at any newspaper will confirm this power. Women are suing men they say "violated" them in some way, and they are doing this at a record pace. Even gay men are getting into the act by suing fellow gays for violating whatever it is that gay men do.

The President of the United States, Donald Trump at the moment, is not the only one under fire. But he has been named by what the newspapers say is a popular, and quite pretty "porn star" during this mad rush to either make money or punish a man. She, the well known porn star, says the President made "repeated calls" to her, and she also said he "hugged" her and two of her friends in his hotel room. The President thus joins what is probably a long list of men who have at least hugged her, considering the business she's in. And maybe even far more, while she was on, or off screen.

That isn't our business.   It is the President's business.

And if the President sues me for even mentioning this, something that is not very likely or logical when you compare our bank accounts, this book will at least become a best seller. But I still support President Trump in the difficult job he has taken on, so I hope not.

Meanwhile, a joke is often a good way to start a book. I've written a few books, so you would think I should know. Used this way, a joke is an attempt by an author to capture and hold a reader's interest and attention, to get the reader "into" the book. Since the author of this book is way older than he looks, and has written over two hundred other books about a great number of subjects, he feels relatively qualified to speak, or, in this case, write. And since in this day and age "the power that women have over men" is something we read about in newspapers and social media every day, it is possible that this joke will hold your interest.

So let's see if a mildly amusing joke can actually pull you into a book. At least try to enjoy the upcoming joke, even if you decide to toss the book, which possibly more than a few readers have done with this author's books.

Here's the joke.

"There is a brand new store that just opened in Canada, where a woman may go to *purchase* a *husband*. Among the instructions on a sign at the entrance to the store is a list of rules that must be followed outlining how the store operates.

"Admission is free," announces the sign at the front door, "but you may go into this store ONLY ONCE! There are six floors in the building," the sign continues, "and the 'value' and 'cost' of the 'husbands' increase as the shopper ascends to the next floor. The shopper may choose any item from any particular floor, and credit cards are accepted. Or the shopper may choose to go up to the next floor, but *may not* go back down except to exit the building, with or without a purchase.

"So this woman goes to the unique store to shop for a husband. On the first floor, the sign on the entry door reads: 'THE MEN ON THIS FLOOR ALL HAVE JOBS.'

"The woman who is 'shopping for a husband' is intrigued, aware that these 'husbands' would at least be the cheapest ones to buy, but she decides to continue up to the second floor, knowing she cannot go back down. On the second floor, a sign at the entrance reads 'THE MEN ON THIS FLOOR ALL HAVE JOBS AND LOVE CHILDREN.'

"That's nice," she agrees, 'but I want more,' so she continues up to the third floor, where the sign reads, 'THE MEN ON THIS FLOOR ALL HAVE JOBS, LOVE CHILDREN, AND ARE VERY GOOD LOOKING.'

"Wow!" she thinks, but she feels the urge to keep going.

"On the fourth floor, the sign before the entry door reads, 'THE MEN ON THIS FLOOR ALL HAVE JOBS, LOVE CHILDREN, ARE VERY GOOD LOOKING, AND ENJOY HELPING WITH THE HOUSEWORK.'

"Oh Mercy me!'" she says out loud, 'I can hardly stand it!'"

"Up she goes to the fifth floor, where the sign reads, 'THE MEN ON THIS FLOOR HAVE JOBS, LOVE CHILDREN, ARE VERY GOOD LOOKING, ENJOY HELPING WITH THE HOUSEWORK, AND HAVE A VERY STRONG ROMANTIC STREAK.'

"She is certainly tempted to shop on this floor, but things are going so well and she has some money in the bank so she decides to go all the way, up to the sixth floor."

"Again there is a sign at the entry door. It says, 'YOU ARE VISITOR NUMBER 31,456,976 TO THIS FLOOR. THERE ARE NO MEN ON THIS FLOOR. THIS FLOOR EXISTS ONLY AS POSITIVE PROOF THAT WOMEN ARE IMPOSSIBLE TO PLEASE. THANK YOU FOR SHOPPING AT THE 'HUSBAND STORE.'

PLEASE USE THE 'EXIT' DOOR, AND HAVE A NICE DAY"

Pretty amusing, eh? But there is more to the joke, so read on.

"Very soon, however, the owner of the 'Husband Store,' to avoid what he is sure would be the almost certain 'gender bias' charges we are all bombarded with on social media every day…charges that could result from the sixth floor sign…decides to open a brand new six floor 'Wive's Store' across the street from his 'Husband Store.' And, yes, there is a sign at the entrance for men seeking a wife.

"THE FIRST FLOOR OF THIS STORE HAS WIVES WHO LOVE SEX.

"The second floor of the new store has a sign at the entry door that announces, 'THE SECOND FLOOR OF THIS STORE HAS WIVES WHO LOVE SEX AND ALSO LOVE BEER.

Please note, the sign continues, 'THE THIRD, FOURTH, FIFTH AND SIXTH FLOORS OF THIS STORE HAVE NEVER BEEN VISITED."

Are you still with me? I have an interesting story to tell, so I hope you are. I, the author of this book, could be threatened with jail myself in view of what is going on today in the United States, although what I'm going to tell you about is well into the past now.

But it did happen, and it is the truth. And it might give you a chuckle.

Did I enjoy it when it was happening? It was so long ago that I don't remember, but I'm guessing probably not. It happened in a frantic few seconds during a somewhat frantic moment that involved a very innocent me and an equally innocent fellow worker, a female worker, at a TV station.

But it has made me think, and even possibly reconsider, many of my thoughts on what is happening now, today, in the sexual harassment field.

Chapter Two

What I'm writing about did happen a number of years ago, although some find that difficult to believe since the author of this book is relatively well known as the author of over two hundred other books, some of them quite readable. The author was, back then and for a short period of time, the host of a television show where a few quite pretty women were hired almost week by week as "co-hosts" to work with him on the show. Some of these nice girls had done this kind of work before, others had not, but who really cared anyhow? The show was not that big a deal and boasted a relatively small audience. And since I was younger then and already involved, I wasn't even looking around for a companion.

In case you are wondering, it is sadly true that when you see the "author" of "over two hundred books" fooling around with a small town TV show instead of at home in his office writing, you can pretty quickly bet that he has a large ego, and that none of his books have become best sellers. In my case, both are sad but also true. You'd think that in all those books, a few thousand readers would have liked at least one or two of them enough to boost sales to some positive consideration by reviewers.

But what the heck, I was keeping the bills paid working as a writer, and even Charles Dickens, an author I greatly admire and even visited once at his grave in Westminster Abbey in London, is said to have struggled for a time before he wrote his marvelous "A Christmas Carol." And, for that matter, he wrote several other books that have become equally famous. Most of Dickens' books are now locked into the history of many generations, not that I am presuming to compare my work with that of my idol, Charles Dickens.

Just to be sure that you don't see this as simply bragging about my "show business" career, what I am about to describe happened while I was hosting the TV show in a smaller town with, probably, a smaller audience. If, that is, whatever audience we had wanted to watch a mid-morning television show, when most folks are at work.

Meanwhile, the ladies hired to work on the show with me, probably to add a little beauty to the set, always did their best even if it was somewhat nervously, and I helped them whenever and wherever I could with my vast knowledge of television show hosting.

A couple of months, actually. And it never occurred to me to hit on any of these ladies in any way at all. I played it absolutely straight with every single one of them. No fooling around on the set. That was the TV station's rules, rules that I was happy to follow, and years before the current situation with women suing men every day for sexual misconduct. Besides, some of those on the crew were quite jealous of my position as "host," and I had to be careful. I wanted them to show me in the best light possible, since they were really in command of the show, and the cameras.

It is also important to understand that I didn't really know any of these ladies very well. We worked together on the show, but that was it. In those days, and maybe still today, it was "five…four…three…and then silently, with fingers, "two…one…" and the cameraman and/or director, depending on who was working that day on the rather small crew, was pointing at us.

That means, to an old radio show host, as I also was for awhile, *you're on the air.*" On TV, it mean's something like "the camera's are rolling."

Still I tried hard to do a good job with the show even though the market was small, and the pay was minimal. But what I am about to tell you would probably get me hauled off to jail, or at least involved in a lawsuit in court, in view of the current "hang 'em at the airport whether they are guilty or not" situation between men and women in the United States today, and certainly including the current feeling that you are "guilty" until you are proven "innocent." That's why I'm not mentioning names of the ladies involved, if I could even remember the names, which I can't. I don't even remember the name the producers used for the show in their advertising, in their effort to build a larger audience.

And all I really remember about my very pretty co-host that day is that she was quite lovely, and a real genuine sweetheart for what she did, and then what she said.

In fact, what I did on the spur of the moment that morning did, all those years ago, get me invited into the boss's office for a lecture on how to treat women on the set. This was even back before the rush by women to get what some of them think they deserve, and what some of them almost certainly do deserve, depending on the situation between them and the men involved. Of somewhat greater importance, the lecture from the boss stressed how *not* to treat women co-workers. The boss did a good job lecturing, even though I wondered throughout the half-hour long meeting why I was alone in his office, and why this wasn't a "staff meeting" for the entire crew. But I still didn't know at that time in his office about the photograph that some jerk in the audience, or on the crew, snapped. And at least the boss, who was an otherwise pretty nice, likeable guy, didn't show me any dirty pictures to illustrate his points during his lecture. He didn't show me the photograph in question either.

I wish he had, since that would have cleared the air very quickly.

How far can we modern men go in today's sexually oriented climate? I just recently, in view of the direction men and women are taking now with the filing of charges about sexual things, corrected a very neat sales lady at a local department store. She was a very attractive lady who was leaning over to better show me a small item I was considering buying. At that moment, I was holding the item in my hand.

My *God*, her breast was within *inches* of my hand there on the counter, I suddenly realized. I had to speak up.

So I cautioned her with a kind word and a smile, and even in a joking way in view of, once again, the situation we modern men find ourselves in today. I turned the situation into a gentle joke. She quickly pulled back. I spoke to her with humor and good will, but I didn't want to be accused of "groping." She was cool, she was polite, she was pleasant, even understanding, as she pulled her breast back.

We both relaxed, although she may have been deep down considering me as some kind of a "weirdo," and hoped only to complete the sale and watch me walk away. But getting back to my main story…

On the day of the modest TV show we are discussing, the jerk in the audience violated the rules and took a photo of us just as my pretty co-host was turning to me in a panic. The countdown had started, the crew was ready, I was ready, and she had fumbled trying to get her lavaliere microphone hooked to her rather loose but otherwise very pretty blouse. This is a microphone that is more or less hidden, with the wire *under* the clothing and with the microphone hooked on clothing closer to the voice of the one doing the speaking.

Please allow me to make one thing clear. I had not even looked at her breasts, or even very closely at her, in the pre-show activity. She was pretty, I remember, and had a smooth voice. At her young age, maybe twenty or twenty one, she probably had the neatest, cutest breasts you can imagine, but at that instant she turned to me in a near-panic and handed me her lavaliere at the end of the wire.

"Help me," she said. "I can't seem to get this hooked up."

Meanwhile, the crew was down to "four" and they were all ready. I was ready, with my opening remarks, ready as always to make it sound like this was just another rather routine show about which I was perfectly confident. In fact, generally speaking, I was always rather confident. Hey, I had been on weekly TV for a couple of months, and with that kind of experience, I knew I was actually pretty good at hosting a TV show.

Maybe even better than I was at writing a book, I have to admit. I was well aware that I hadn't yet been really "discovered" as a writer of books, but maybe I would be as a TV host in Southern California. Some producer out there might be at that very moment trying to find the world's next

"Johnny Carson" when he stumbled across our show.

There was only one way to handle the problem of the "wandering lavaliere" microphone without starting over with the whole procedure for the crew.

"Lean forward," I ordered as politely as I could.

She did.

Very quickly I reached up under her sagging blouse, aimed the microphone at the "V" at her throat, hooked up the lavaliere in its correct location on her blouse with the microphone clip, and then withdrew my hand. It took a second, two at the most. I may not be all that great as a writer or a TV host, but I am dynamite at hooking up microphones when the count is on and only seconds remain.

"Three!" The crew could see what was happening but the count had continued. And I wasn't giving a single, even random thought to what were probably the very cute, perhaps even "perky" breasts, under her blouse. Not a thought.

"Two," the crew waved.

Then "One" with another wave of the hand, showing one finger, with several of the crew helping to be sure I saw them. There was no more time, but we were by then ready.

Before they could point, meaning "on air," I heard her whisper *"Thanks, and you were a perfect gentleman."*

That was it. The microphone was in place, she was calm, more or less, and the show went on. And the name of the guy in the audience, or on the crew, who snapped the photo, even though it was not really permitted, has been lost in history.

All I really know for sure is that he passed the developed photo back to the crew, who later showed it to me, and I realized that it is a photo that may show up one day, sooner or later, somewhere or other, probably when I have decided to run for some very important elective office like City Council or something. I promise you that if I had it, I would use it here, in this book, as an illustration, since I can for the first time explain it, including what she said about my manners. And if the one who shot the photo is reading this and still has a copy, I will give you prominent credit in this book if you permit me to use it, and we'll all forget about what the past mistakenly implies.

The photo probably still exists these years later. It could eventually come back to haunt me, or maybe it will surface long after I am gone, but in that case it will be exhibited with no further explanation, including what she said about "a perfect gentleman," to even haunt my grandchildren.

Not that an explanation is really needed. What is happening on the set in the photo is quite obvious and very, very clear. There I am, with my hand up under her blouse, and with a warm smile on my face. There is as I recall only panic on her face which, now that I think about it, is quite logical in view of what seems to be happening to her. She has, from all appearances, become the first show business personality in the modern mad rush to have been "groped" by another member of the cast of a TV show. I saw the snapshot a week later and the crew, and I, had a great laugh over it at first. There was no doubt. There I was, easy to identify, with my hand up inside the blouse of a fellow host, a *female* host. And what am I doing? I'm staring down happily at the well hidden breasts I appear to be fondling.

Only when I saw the photo did I understand why I was called in for a lecture from the boss, an otherwise very intelligent man who apparently just took one look at the photo and acted, as any good boss should act. But he acted without even hearing the heartfelt, "You were a perfect gentleman," after my reaching up under her blouse to hook up the microphone as the count was going down.

And if the boss from back then happens to be reading this book, and wants to offer a few words of apology, or something or other, he can sure give me a call. I'm easy to find.

So today, in view of what is happening between men and women, and courts of law, I often think back to that day, and pause before I shout in my mind to "*hang the dirty old man*" who has been accused, but not convicted, of sexual misconduct. I was as innocent of "groping" as I could possibly be, and in fact not a person suggested this, but the photo shot by the jerk among the audience or the crew, certainly says otherwise. It does appear that I am fondling a fellow performer's breasts, with or without her permission, not that it matters under those circumstances on a TV show set. I appear to be as guilty as sin.

And it never occurred to me on that day to be anything but a gentleman under those circumstances. The cameras were an instant from rolling. I did what I thought was needed, and it worked, and that was that. We had a guest waiting to be interviewed, and we did that rather well, I recall. Later, after the show, she again said, "You really got me out of a tough spot, and I appreciate it. They could have fired me for not being ready, but you were there to help. And as I said before, you were a perfect gentleman." Or at least words to the effect.

In other words, I didn't even slightly touch any forbidden…well…you know…*sensitive*, places.

Today that could have started anything from a "I have been touched without my permission and I want to protest," to "I have been touched without my permission, and much worse, and I want *revenge, or at least some real money!*" Since it seems to take forever now for things to work their way through a court of law, I probably won't live, at my advanced age, to see the final acts in several of these modern dramas you already know about. I was pretty old back then, I am way older now.

But I hate to miss these legal conclusions, because I am just as confused as everyone else. Let's break it down before we get into details about who has been accused of doing what, and when it happened, and who was really hurt. First of all, being a straight man for my whole life and one who appreciates women as co-workers and friends and even closer, it is very difficult for me, personally (and this is true for other men I have interviewed), to understand how a one man alone in a "rape" situation can even manage.

I know it must happen because we read about these foul acts in almost every morning newspaper almost every day, but what I and the guys I interviewed have difficulty understanding is how a man can...well...*perform*, under such unpleasant, demanding, sometimes even screaming, very high pressure situations? The guys I talked to felt sure that getting a...well, you know, getting *ready,* seems to them to be almost impossible when the one you are with is neither cooperating nor cooperative. You are doing something against her will, unless you are threatening to kill her children or do some other horrible thing if she doesn't cooperate. So of course rape does happen, and has happened throughout history, but the guys I talked to agreed that it seemed impossible. Some of them also pointed out, though, that the act of rape is not so much sexual as it is a need, a demand, for power over another individual. Also difficult for most of us to understand, but then most of us have never raped anyone.

Then there are also the dozens of women involved in these dramas. Yes, some of them are desperate for a role in a film, or in some other "on stage" position. Some of them might have very willingly "given in" to a prominent producer who could make their career dreams come true. To some of them, this might just be another, even better way to make money. Some of them may already be accustomed to giving sexual favors for career enhancement. Some of them might even have suggested this "trade." or hinted at it. Some of them might even have jumped at the chance to perform for a producer or director before any on-stage performance.

When a powerful producer or director demands sex from a lower ranking person in order for that person to be considered for a part in a play or motion picture, or just a favor at work, sometimes that person cooperates and does as the producer or director demands. And very often they do get the part or the favor. They know they must do one thing, and that is to make a part of their body available to the higher ranking person. So they do something they may have done many times before but under more pleasant circumstances. They do make their body available knowing they are not necessarily going to enjoy the act, and so they get the part or the favor. The young lower ranking man or woman who refused to cooperate didn't get the part, and life goes on. Nobody gets really hurt, other than a shock to the "freedom to do as only you choose to do" part of your life.

In two newspapers in the first week of 2018, there were two separate stories about sexual misconduct. One, in the Ventura County Star in Ventura, California, and credited to the Associated Press and USA Today, reported about lawyers paying off a porn star for something that happened with the President of the United States. The other paper reported about the civil lawsuit that has been filed by a "publicist" against Oscar-winning filmmaker and noted screenwriter-director Paul Haggis, whose work includes the well-known "Million Dollar Baby," starring prominent actors Clint Eastwood and Hillary Swank. Swank, who seemed taken aback by the filings, said on the internet that she was "stunned" at the legal action against Haggis, who also wrote and directed "Crash," starring equally prominent actors Don Cheadle and Sandra Bullock.

The story in the papers reported that the publicist said Haggis forced her to perform oral sex and then raped her. Immediately three other women filed similar lawsuits against the writer/director, generally claiming that Haggis "first tried to kiss them," then, in all three of the cases, "when they fought back, he escalated his aggression."

"I need to be inside you," one of the women filing said that Haggis said to her before she "managed to run away." This is pretty much to the point, but not beyond what many men have said to a woman they desire although usually in a very loving way and only if they have the nerve to say what they are thinking. The lawyer representing Haggis insists that he "didn't rape anybody," and also reports that one of the accuser's, and her lawyer, demanded a payment of nine million dollars to avoid legal action.

We can all keep an eye on the newspapers as this plows its way through several courts, if it ever gets to the courts. More likely, it will be settled, and for quite a bit less money.

Is this extortion, or rape? Did Haggis do wrong, or not? Most of us believe what we read in respected newspapers, but what more is there to stories like this? Has a crime been committed, nor not? Should someone be in jail, or not? That's why the author would like to see why the increasing number of "sexually aggressive" situations are settled for a sum of money rather than a jail term for a crime. We'll get to the second story in a moment.

The author, again many years ago but to show how legal matters are nerve-wracking and can even effect health, was once sued by an almost unknown person for something the author had written. He originally wrote the story in question for "True Magazine," a respected and very popular magazine of a number of years ago.

The story was, at that point, a career-changing victory for a young writer.

Anyhow, to get to the point, I proposed a story to the magazine's editor, which is the way we did things back then to make a living. The story was to be about a man who claimed to be the "reincarnation" of William Bonney, better known as "Billy the Kid." Reincarnation and regression by hypnosis was very big back then, and this guy had said he had been sent back by hypnosis while in prison, done by a prison hypnotist, to a previous life; he was at that time a recently released convict for some charge or other. He was willing, even anxious, to cooperate when I contacted him, and to be sent back again while we, a photographer and I, watched. The photographer took photos of him in a sound-proof room so that we could watch what was happening as he went "back" to his previous existence as "Billy," but we could not hear what the hypnotist was saying so we wouldn't be hypnotized ourselves into believing a bunch of baloney. Yeah, we were being very careful, but I was aiming high since I had sent the proposal to one of the top magazines of the day, and it would be a solid boost to my writing career to be published by True Magazine.

Non-believers of this hypnotic technique generally called the whole idea of "regression" dumb, and suggested that only strong believers in reincarnation, as well as the commanding voice of a hypnotist, really believed this technique could work. Our guy did strongly believe that he was the reincarnation of "The Kid," and hoped that my story in True Magazine would convince others. Most of these "others" generally just made fun of him and his odd beliefs.

One of the problems with being a free lance writer is that an editor of a very popular magazine may, for any reason at all, use his power to reject a story. Even a story he has approved as an idea. And True Magazine editor's, while I was in my own mind spending the almost certain thousand dollar check I was going to get, did reject the story. I believe the word they used was "unbelievable." Before my regular stories in Reader's Digest, which was a much higher paying market, True Magazine was the most generous magazine I had tried for. It was very near the top in free lance markets.

But my dream was over. The editor had rejected my story. I wouldn't be in "True," as much as I wanted to be there.

This did not, however, end the story. Not by a very long shot. The unhappiest part, in fact, is still to come.

I had an agent back then, and he enjoyed the "Billy the Kid Returns" story. He tried to market it again and again, and finally did manage to place it in a third or fourth rate magazine that paid me a hundred or so dollars to publish it. And I had to give a percentage of that money to both the agent and the photographer. All things considered, I just wished by then that The Kid would go away.

End of story?

Oh no, not even yet.

A couple of years later, after the story was published in the second rate magazine, and although I had no knowledge whatever of this, "The "Kid" had apparently found religion, but had then been according to reports from lawyers, rejected by his church, the members of which did not know he was a former convict. I'm told they had learned of this past life of his only through my story in the questionable magazine. For that matter, what these folks in that seriously religious church were doing reading a "men's" magazine of this quality is quite beyond me, and also what any of this has to do with religion, which I have always understood indicated forgiving people, I have no idea. For that matter I'm not a very religious person myself, and, heck, I would forgive some writer who made a few bucks with a story about myself that I was anxious to have published. But this church saw that the magazine featured mildly pretty ladies who were nearly naked, and that, from what I am told, really offended them. The photos had nothing to do with the regression story, and didn't offend me in the slightest, although most of them did look like ladies who might have been rejected by "Playboy" for sagging breasts or inadequate buttocks. But the magazine's modest check, when it finally arrived many weeks later. was welcome in my household, and my bank accepted it.

End of story, finally.

No, not at all.

After yet another years long period of time, "The Kid" decided to sue me, and for the back-breaking amount of one hundred twenty five thousand dollars, for writing the story and not getting it published in True Magazine. He probably found a lawyer who needed money, and who told him he "had an airtight case" against me, certain to bring in thousands for both of them.

Permit me, if you will, to ask you to temporarily change places with me for just a moment. Put yourself in my place if you will, still a mildly struggling writer with a few credits in some magazines that most people would not even look at on the racks of the local newsstand for fear that someone they know might see them, but a writer still barely making a living.

By then, in fact, I had pretty much forgotten about Billy and his story...I hadn't heard from him in years, and the story was long ago published...but the guy came to my door with the legal papers and informed me that I was being sued.

OK, "Billy The Kid" had decided to sue me, and for the stunning amount of one hundred twenty five thousand dollars, a gigantic amount of money in those days. This was being done because I wrote the story that what the lawyers said got him kicked out of his church, and then for not getting it published in True Magazine. I had told him that "True" was the magazine who had expressed interest in the story, I admit. In fact, I was proud to admit that, back then.

But also back then, one hundred twenty five thousand dollars was a small fortune, and to me, a still somewhat struggling writer, it was a "big" fortune. By then I was more than paying the bills as a writer of magazine stories, and I had moved to California "where the writers live," but that was a *ton* of money I did not have. I had a home I was buying in a better section of Los Angles, a few dollars in the bank, and some editors who seemed to like my work.

Of course I had to hire a lawyer, since that is all a part of the system, and my lawyer smiled and said "Don't worry too much about this. They'll want to settle."

Don't worry?

He had to be kidding! How would you feel if you were being sued by someone you can barely remember for something you had nothing to do with, and for a mountain of money, as more and more men are facing today. What I mean is, in the hundreds of lawsuits being filed or at least being considered, it is just possible that some of these guys "didn't do it."

This lawsuit with "The Kid" began my sleepless nights, and my worries by day. It was on my mind constantly. I was having difficulty working. My family was worried. Were we headed for the poor house? That is, for most normal people, a pretty standard reaction from one who is being sued, as so many men are being sued now.

Even the conclusion of this crazy legal situation was nerve-wracking for a man who loses sleep over a parking ticket. After a year or so of nothing but worry, and my ducking out of meetings with the other side whenever I could, on a day like any other day except that the heavy "lawsuit yolk" was lifted from my shoulders, my lawyer called with what he considered to be good news.

"They seriously want to settle," he said, happily I thought, although the longer this went on, the more money he was in line to make. This still didn't make much of an impression on me because all I could see in "settling" a gigantic lawsuit like this had to involve thousands of dollars and would be what would probably still be back-breaking. I hemmed and hawed and finally asked, "Yeah, for how much?"

Then the sun came out.

The weight floated from my shoulders completely. This happened the instant he spoke.

"Two hundred dollars," he said, perfectly seriously.

I asked him to repeat the amount. He did. "Two hundred dollars."

"That's great…just…great…" I said, almost through tears.

"I turned them down, of course," he then announced. "I knew you would agree with this decision I made."

One hundred twenty five thousand dollars would still have been kind of tough for me, and probably for many of us, to scrape up and then just give away, but two hundred dollars was easily worth getting some sleep at night and thinking about other things during the day. Even though I felt the lawsuit was groundless, and a waste of everyone's time, two hundred bucks sounded *wonderful*.

And my lawyer had turned it down.

"Why…?" was all I could think of to say.

"I think I can get them down a little bit more. This was just their first offer."

We finally settled on one hundred twenty five dollars. *One hundred twenty five lousy dollars!* Even someone begging on the street can probably come up with that amount in an emergency. And I had been losing sleep for months, for years, in fact.

Even now, though, I remember that I did sleep better that night. I wrote the check to "The Kid," my bank honored it when the other side brought it in, and the lawsuit was done. I was in for a couple of thousand in legal fees, but that which had been dragging on me for years was lifted. I was *free!*

Lawsuits are a real burden for almost everyone. You may have enough money to just hand things over to your lawyer, as many of the men in today's lawsuits are, but they are probably even a burden for a very rich person. They are certainly a burden for some of the entertainers mentioned in the current flock of lawsuits being filed. These guys have money, but it is money they would prefer to keep, and with some of them it seems they just picked the wrong time to make a move on a woman, and so the "piper must be paid."

One way or another, with cash if you are rich, with jail of you are not. Or so the accusers are threatening.

Even over in our friendly/enemy, China, sex and sex education can be a problem, and every Friday a special teacher in a special classroom at Tongxin Experimental School, discusses sex with the students who are children of migrant workers. This teacher's lectures cover subjects like how a student should prevent sexual assault. This has happened because of the kindergarten abuse scandals that recently created a public rage in China. In fact, it seems like Chinese parents over there love their children just as much as we in this country love our children.

According to a story in many U.S. newspapers in early 2018, the teacher, Li Xueyan, might say to the class, "And if your internet friend asks to meet you alone in person, what do you say?"

"No!!" the young students respond with a shout. This is one result of what happened recently in China, where the country was shocked by the multiple kindergarten abuse scandals that all the newspapers covered, including an especially serious one in Beijing, in a report involving sleeping pills and suspicious "health checkups" for the children. Now, sex education is a new interest among parents of younger children in that country, as Chinese parents search for how such abuse can be prevented.

Even though an "Official Investigation" reported that no sexual abuse had occurred in the Beijing incident, frightened parents in China are taking the matter into their own hands, and demanding answers.

In Syria, where gender rights have been in question for centuries, Ibrahim Habloush, who is living with his family of ten in a windswept desert camp in the northwestern part of the country, a camp that has been set up for people displaced by the fight against Islamic State extremists, there are problems. According to Ibrahim, "They give a lot of of rights to women. If I raise my voice to a woman, they might put me in jail."

Join the crowd in the United States, Ibrahim. We "modern men" are being way more careful that we used to be.

The world is learning what the United States is learning, that women have rights and the time has come for them to express these rights. Ibrahim further reports that when some of the men in the camp complained to their leaders, they were told "Sorry, we have a *democracy* now."

Ibrahim's camp is run by ethnic Kurdish forces who apparently have some distinctly progressive ideas about the rights of women. Many women in the United States think that some of the ideas aren't bad at all.

Chapter Three

But before you read one more word in this book, it is time to take a hard look at exactly what is happening every day, and reported in almost every newspaper or on every television station very quickly, most often with at least one very famous person involved. What is the truth, and what isn't?

What can we believe?

Meanwhile, some woman is suing some man for something, generally having to do with sex, almost every day. Or some man, probably a well-known man, is paying off some woman "to keep her mouth shut" about some sexual misadventure. Or at least some gay man is suing some other gay man because the second one slapped the first one on the back in greeting, and the lawsuit says the second one "attacked" the first one, and "struck" him. Which, if everyone is telling the truth, is…well…true.

We men won't be able to slap another man on the back from now on. That is illegal, and you can ask any lawyer (who will probably take your case to make a few bucks before you settle over this perfectly innocent act of friendship). Let's go all the way back to the top, to the President of the United States, Donald Trump himself at the time of this writing, since he is probably the most powerful man in the world. There was a story in a respected west coast newspaper apparently written by "Heidi" something or other, and credited to "USA TODAY" and "The Wall Street Journal." *"Heidi"* is probably just a reporter and almost certainly without immediate access to the President, but the story is just too good to ignore because of what it *really* says. The author took the time to ask a lawyer to read and carefully study the story in the newspaper, since it was short and appeared to be to the point.

He then asked for a comment from the legal expert."It means nothing at all, the way it is written.," said the lawyer. The story, the lawyer agreed, was baseless, useless, meaningless, a waste of space. "It means nothing at all," the lawyer repeated. We all know that President Trump sometimes goes off the deep end, more often than not with "tweets," and we all pray that he doesn't press any buttons on his desk during one of the times when he is "off" that deep end. Otherwise, many of us still support him because we have all, upon some occasion, lost our cool and we have all occasionally misplaced our temper. We have all become upset, angry about something, or just "lost our temper" and said or did something in a moment of anger that we wish we could take back two seconds later. But if you or I say something, not that many, and certainly not that many newspaper reporters, pay much attention. But when the *President* says something, good or bad, it is instantly *NEWS*. That, in fact, is one of the toughest things about being President of the United States. He can't say a word without it being reported as "absolute truth" in the newspapers. Here's what the story in the respected west coast newspaper said in the opening paragraph, the "lead" of the story, to get your attention. This is exactly as it was printed in the paper, the local paper and probably the big, major USA Today newspaper.

"A lawyer representing President Donald Trump arranged a $130,000 payment to a former adult film star one month before the 2016 presidential election to prevent her from discussing an alleged sexual encounter between her and Trump a decade earlier, The Wall Street Journal reported. Pretty heavy stuff, in view of the fact that he was a candidate for the highest office in the world at that time. He was running for the office of President of the United States with a reasonable chance of winning against Hillary Clinton. Many even thought he *would* win, and others thought he had a good chance of winning. He did win, as we all now know, and took on what many consider a "thankless" job that automatically ages a man, and turns his hair white.

We all know that many of us read only the headline and the lead paragraph and then move on to other stories. We also know that at least some of us men, very few of us of course, have, way back in our youth, maybe, actually paid a girl to do something nice to us, or with us. And with things as they are in the sexual area in the country today, most of us would say about the apparent antics of the President,

"Well, OK, I guess," and move on. The President is vastly wealthy. He can afford a porn star as lovely as this one seems to be in photographs, and probably also was quite lovely a few months ago, when this was reported..

So what's the big deal?

To be perfectly straight, and to cover every base in this "story,' the headline at the top said this.

"Report: Lawyer for Trump paid porn star."

OK, most of us would not expect the man who was planning to become President of the United States to go visit the "star" of pornographic films to carry a check for a large amount of money to not talk about an "alleged sexual encounter." He would order one of his associates to do this job, and in this case that could apparently be what this lawyer did do for him.

But "apparently" is another of those "soft" words that means almost nothing. Soft words like "apparently" and "alleged" should not be used in newspapers. They are really great words for reporters, and are meant to be broad and even misleading, but they are not "hard words."

Let's break it down in our effort to be straight and honest. Even the story in the local paper, The Ventura County Star on January 14, 2018, with credit to both "USA Today" and "The Wall Street Journal," admitted that the sexual encounter was "alleged" to have happened. Alleged, according to the Internet, means "supposed" and "suspected" and "so-called" and "assumed" and also, of course, "alleged." None of these words are solid, hard words. All are "maybe" words, and none are "true" words like "kill" or "sell" or, well, you get the picture. There is more to this story if you are interested. The Wall Street Journal cited "anonymous" sources who were "familiar with the matter." Anonymous, on the Internet, can mean "nameless" or "unidentified" or "unnamed" or "unsigned" or "unspecified" or "unknown" or "secret" or even "shadowy" or "mysterious." "Familiar" can mean almost anything at all, depending on what you are trying to say.

And the story also pointed out that the woman in the matter in question, Stephanie Clifford, known in her porn films as "Stormy Daniels," did not comment directly with the Wall Street Journal and also that President Trump's longtime lawyer, "declined to comment." So what really happened? Who knows?

Miss Daniels is quoted in the story as saying "Rumors that I have received hush money from Donald Trump are completely false. If indeed I did have a relationship with Donald Trump, trust me, you wouldn't be reading about it in the news, you would be reading about it in my book. But the fact of the matter is, these stories are not true."

And that could be the problem with almost all of these sexual reports that are leading to court actions. None of them seem to name specific names or discuss specific crimes or talk about when and where and how the accusers were violated, if they were violated. But if they were violated, it is a crime. So maybe they are just in the game for a settlement. They all have lawyers, and lawyers should know the law, and are in business to make money.

Since the story also said, "Clifford did not comment directly to the Journal," most readers are probably discounting the whole story. But it was amusing, and interesting, for a moment or two.

Let's forget the stuff about Clifford and her book which, if someone handed her a check for over a hundred thousand dollars, she doesn't even have to write. And if they didn't hand her a check to keep quiet, she has far more interesting things to write about in any book.

Many readers are doing just that, chuckling at the paper and forgetting the "story." And certainly the President of the United States has far more important things to think about.

Chapter Four

Then there is the "youth coach" in Los Angles who has fallen from "hero" to "potential defendant." He is an Olympic gold medal winning boxer in East Los Angeles and a real genuine "celebrity" to his thousands of fans. But he now faces counts of "lewd acts with a child" after allegedly "grooming" a thirteen year old girl and molesting her while she was one of his young students.

A family member of the girl is said to have reported the accused young teacher/boxer to the Los Angles County Sheriff's Office.

Significantly, he is also charged with possessing child pornography, according to the police and the media. This is something that the men interviewed for this book find very difficult to comprehend.

"Who wants to look at dirty pictures of kids?" was their almost certain and almost universal response.

"And how can a child's photographs possibly be pornographic?" was another popular response.

But child pornography does exist, and where most men, even men who have found some enjoyment from porn in their life, have little interest in this bottom of the heap, "child" level. The author of this book originally planned to go to the Internet and offer some reasonable examples here, but finally decided against doing so for a specific reason beyond that of just making him sick. In case he goes out and robs a bank, or does some other really dumb thing, he doesn't want anything like that in his computer when the police check it, as they always do. Child pornography is a very special type of sick crime that some rare men seek out, for whatever their warped reasons.

The Los Angeles County Sheriff's department, according to Lt. Todd Deeds in the Los Angeles Times, said, "investigators have no specific information that (the accused boxer) molested others, but given his extensive contact with youth, we are very concerned that there are more victims out there."

OK. Most of us agree that policeman have the right and duty to search for "more victims" in a crime case. That is their job, and most of us hope they do the job with gusto. But still that "have no specific information" statement must carry some weight.

One thing does become obvious. The young boxer's life is ruined. It will take him years to recover from this "search for more victims," which will necessarily keep the case alive and of interest to newspapers. And perhaps this is exactly what he deserves. He was a teacher of kids. If you were a parent, would you turn your little daughter over to him for training, after all that has happened? Probably not, right?

Would you allow him to "groom" your young daughter after what the newspapers have said? Think about this for a moment. At the 1984 Olympics, the U.S. team was packed with boxing talent. Future World Champion Evander Holyfield was on the team, and so was Pernell Whitaker, Meldrick Taylor and Mark Breland on the powerful boxing team. The author, in his work in that '84 Olympics in Los Angeles, had the opportunity to see several of these young boxers in action, including the one discussed here. He won, and deserved, the gold medal. He then went into teaching kids, boys and girls, to box.

The Americans won nine gold medals that year, including the one this young boxer earned. When the Times reported on how the team did, they wrote, "When Los Angeles hosted the 1984 Olympics, few stories were more satisfying for the hometown crowd than this boxer from a Boyle Heights housing project, a twenty year old light flyweight who faced and beat gang violence and poverty and a last minute broken hand (all the way) to gold triumph. The oldest of eight children and raised by a single mother in a housing development, he stood tall on the winner's podium. "As the national anthem played, he, the first Mexican-American to win a gold medal, clenched a small American flag and fought back tears," said the L.A. Times. "Ten years of struggle, and pain, and I'm here," he then said to broadcaster Howard Cosell.

Now, a few years later, whether or not what they are saying, and writing in the newspapers, is true, his teaching career is probably over and his future is black. Does he even really understand that what he is accused of doing, and perhaps did do? Does he know it was a crime, if he did it?

Does the "prince of the barrio," as he was called throughout most of his training days, realize what is happening? They won't be calling him for motivational speeches in poorer sections of town and around the country anymore. Now reporters will be shoving microphones at him for explanations. His reputation as a community hero has been trashed. Guilty or not, he is ruined.

But he is a fighter, and although his boxing days may be over, he could decide to fight back on these charges. Sooner or later, someone is certainly going to fight back, guilty or not, in view of what is happening with lawsuits being filed and newspapers eating up the details. In court you must prove things, and some of these things are very hard not only to talk about, but to prove.

Chapter Five

Let's not forget disgraced former Olympic doctor Larry Nassar. Nearly one hundred women and girls recently spoke or had their statements read during a four-day-long hearing in Lansing, Michigan. Many of them were crying and all of them were speaking on the terrible effects of what the former doctor had done to them during his time as an Olympic team doctor, and what he had inflicted on them back when they were children.

This was a "sentencing" hearing. The doctor had been found guilty, unlike many of the current lawsuits that are still winding their way through courts. Some of the now-adult women in the Lansing court asked that their identifications be withheld, others spoke out strongly against Nassar.

Judge Rosemarie Aquillina softly consoled the women, and repeated that they should not blame themselves. Then she said to the convicted doctor, "I've just signed your 'death warrant.'" She was referring to the *forty to one hundred seventy five years in prison* she had approved as the former doctor's sentence.

But many of us not so deeply involved in this important sporting event are forced to re-think the Olympics, and to re-think about those who are in charge. What if your son or daughter had won a place on one of the Olympic teams? You would without a doubt be proud of your child, and happy for them, and would cheer for them.

This was a doctor who had been approved by the numerous committees who make such choices to medically treat the young female participants. They are trusted absolutely to give this care to the ones who have worked so hard to be there on the teams from many different countries.

It does force many of us to go back to the Olympics of 1972 in Munich, Germany, and the hated "Black September" nickname. It was a sad event that generated the other horrible nickname "Munich Massacre." This was an attack on the athlete's living quarters during the 1972 Summer Olympics, where eleven Israeli Olympic team members were taken hostage and eventually killed, along with a German police officer, by a Palestinian terrorist group. So in spite of the careful "vetting" of associates of teams, mistakes are made, and it is often the athletes like your child who pays.

Meanwhile, getting back to the United States, we have learned from a 2017 release from United States Supreme Court Chief Justice John G. Roberts that even the federal court system does need to look over the rules and procedures to make sure that everyone understands it all if they are being subjected to sexual harassment or other "inappropriate behavior."

"Events in recent months have illuminated the depth of the problem of sexual harassments in the workplace," wrote Chief Justice Roberts in his year end report on the federal judiciary, "and events in the past few weeks have made clear that the judicial bench is not immune." Here he seemed to be referring to veteran Judge Alex Kozinski, of the 9th Circuit Court in California, who recently retired after a series of women reported he had shown them pornography or made sexual comments during their service as law clerks.

Is it OK for a woman, often a woman from a man's past, even distant past, to accuse that man of molesting her at some time during that past? And the "molesting" can be anything from mildly touching her, or even making "joking" suggestions of a sexual nature, or worse, such as touching that is more like an actual grope?"

All the way, in fact, to rape?

OK, OK, that is for a court to decide, right? One thing we can dismiss quickly. Rape is a crime. A woman should not rape a man, and a man should not rape a woman.

If either gender says "No" to the other gender, it means *NO!* The days of the old "yes or no" game playing have passed, probably never to return. But can there be "levels" of rape, which opens a brand new door? If you take her home after a first date, and at the door she says, "I had a really nice time. Goodnight," and you are absolutely certain she is standing just aside enough to mean "Come on in if you want to," should you or shouldn't you "go on in," or should you just go on home? Now, with the way things are, you should probably just go home.

So is it a crime, or is it just the playing of a game between a man and a woman that leads to sex? You know, he or she says "no" but really means "yes." And that probably opens many other doors.

Maybe, maybe not, since the man, and we have dozens of examples of this in our modern world, is pretty much going to be ruined if this happens to him. If he refuses to pay up, he will be taken down. If "paying up" is even possible, though it has happened in a number of modern cases, and perhaps will happen in many more. The trouble is, the man's reputation is probably destroyed, and maybe it should be, whether or not he has actually gone "over the line."

But the problem can be that maybe he doesn't think for an instant that he has gone over that difficult to really see "line." She, in the case of a woman accusing a man, is certain that he has, or at least to the point of accepting a "pay off." He may be shocked, and have no idea that they were only "playing around," and that he would not have gone one tiny step further if he had known he was "assaulting" her.

Or maybe he knows that he has gone too far, but was willing to take the risk, or that sooner or later she would "give in" without further trouble.

At the writing of this book, and you know the names as well as I, the reputations of men are being ruined, and some of them, without a court decision, seem to perhaps deserve it. On the other hand, it hasn't yet been proven in a court of law and at the time of this writing, those men, and for some reason more men in show business, it seems, are prone to say "Hey, beautiful, do me this one little favor and

I'll confirm you for the role you so desperately want."

This "beautiful" one is almost always in the person of a young woman (and they usually are truly beautiful). She may have left home, moved perhaps to Hollywood, maybe with her family and children, and has tried to break in to show business in a play or a night club or a musical or even a radio program. They just need one little "break" to make it to the top. And the one who called them "beautiful" and asked for the "little favor," does have the power to get them the perfect job that will give them the break they need.

And, yes, they are becoming desperate. It can be as bad as trying to break in to be a writer, when everyone in the world thinks they can write a best selling book about their life, and publishers are flooded with manuscripts, most of questionable quality. And many of which, by the way, are more often than not returned unread, if enough postage is included. All this pretty young girl must do to make her dreams come true is one little, tiny "sexual favor" for a man who very often can't get any woman to do anything at all for him unless he pays for it. Most of these men, as you have seen from the frequent photos in the media, are far from being a "Robert Redford" when he was at his best in the looks or age or physique department. They know it, and maybe that's why they take advantage of a young woman trying to survive in what can be a brutal business.

The trouble is, very often this "one little favor" has something to so with sex in some form or other. The man isn't going to ask them to run and get him a cup of coffee. Think about this for a moment. It never occurred to me to touch what must have been the very cute breasts of my TV co-host. Especially not when she needed my help seconds before the camera's "rolled," and not even at some time later. But let's take one more look at this situation. Suppose the one I helped with the lavaliere was perfectly happy with her job as a co-host on a smaller town TV show. Suppose she wanted very much to keep the job, and thought I might be able to help her in ways other than adjusting her microphone, and what if she actually wanted me to touch her, thinking that having me on her side might help down the line. Suppose she was perfectly willing to go "all the way" to keep me on her side.

I'm no Robert Redford, for sure, but just suppose for a moment, although none of these "supposes" are very likely since the host of a smaller town TV show has almost no power at all. Very likely if I had threatened to quit the show, they probably would have said, "Hey, go ahead and quit. Somebody from the crew can take over, and maybe even do a better job."

But with her, my co-host, each one of these stories we read about are different. I don't think so, in her case, but I don't really *know.*

In fact, it is not likely at all I'm quite sure, but keep in mind that this is just supposing. What I do remember about her is that she was very nice, never seemed to kid around with me or the crew, quite lovely, intelligent, and yes, even career-minded. She needed help, I helped her, and that was that.

And I would do it again, even with the jerk in the audience with a camera. Only this time I wouldn't smile.

Try to keep in mind that there many of us men who are the kind of person, as I was, who was disgusted when the guys at the local Press Club insisted that Marilyn Monroe, back in those days, was having an affair with President Kennedy. Why take shots like that, and what possible reason would Monroe have for having sex with the President? She didn't need any help with her career. In fact, she was at the very top, as Mr. Kennedy was at the top. And she was also a very good actress, as motion pictures like "Bus Stop" prove. There is a scene in that movie, very near the end, where the hero whips off his heavy coat and wraps it around her shoulders on an icy cold, snowy morning outside the "bus stop". Her response as he settles the warm jacket around her shoulders…her whispered thanks…has always been, to me and perhaps to show business history, the most feminine scene ever filmed, or that I have ever witnessed in a motion picture by any actress, anywhere, in any movie. Marilyn Monroe was purely and absolutely a *woman* in that brief scene.

You must really see this tender moment to realize what a fine actress Marilyn Monroe was, since it is said that she didn't even like her co-star all that much. In that scene she was just acting, and it seems very *real*. Her fans still miss her today. Her response to the hero's new, improved affection might bring tears to your eyes. Best of all, this film is fun, and moving, and thought provoking, and very entertaining, and has an ending that sneaks up on you, and delights you. Marilyn Monroe's legion of fans, including the author, hopes she is resting in peace after her untimely passing. She was a fine actress who was in great demand in spite of the frequent difficulties she is said to have created on the set of some productions in which she participated. So she didn't learn her lines in time, or is said by other actors to have exhibited temper tantrums often.

So what?

Many of us have been on small town television, but most of us have never been invited to the set of a Marilyn Monroe motion picture, so most of us have no idea about that, including the author.

And back in the Los Angeles Press Club days, I was also disgusted when the guys at the club were passing around stories about Rock Hudson being gay. The fact that this was none of my business, and that Hudson was one of my favorite actors, and that I certainly have nothing against gays except that they seem to have no idea what they are missing, meant little. I just felt that being gay was private business, and shouldn't be bandied about by a number of junior reporters who had no real way of knowing but who still talked like "experts" on almost any subject. It always reminds me, with a smile, of course, of CNN on TV, and the girl reporters who try to sound so "knowledgeable," but often fail, but only because they are girls trying to be boys. How often have you watched a big, important football game, and listened to a female reporter on the sideline? Some jobs are made for men, and some for women, and if you want to call that "gender bias," go ahead. I'm guilty. But it has always seemed to me that these pretty ladies with a high paying job are even trying to *sound* like men by "gruffing up" their voices.

However, in the above cases about Rock Hudson and Marilyn Monroe, and the rumors about them, both rumors, and many other such stories, eventually turned out to be true. Apparently, from recent secret service reports, the affair between Monroe and Kennedy was real, and fine actor Rock Hudson did die of a now-curable disease that at that time and until a while back, did kill many gays.

Chapter Six

The newspapers, and you can believe what you choose to believe about what you read although most of it is probably reasonably true, are sometimes fascinating. They should be read every single morning, at least two of them to get the different points of view of editors. Even though, sadly, the "news" is sometimes directed more at selling newspapers than writing about the real news. But the papers did report around the end of 2015 that a baseball player was being named in the current, at that time, rush to judge men who have stepped "over the line."

Baseball players generally do not look for routine publicity, although perhaps some of them must, to keep their jobs. A baseball player who almost always hits home runs every time he steps to the plate doesn't worry about getting his name in the papers. His name will be there almost every day throughout the season.

This player we are discussing here, and you can look this up, was accused of "assault" against a female photographer while both were at a planned "photo shoot."

Hey, he probably grabbed one of her cameras and hit her over the head, right? She probably bled all over the place, right?

No, but what she said he did do might be considered even worse by women. Or maybe not, especially by men.

At one staged 2015 "autograph session" in Minneapolis, sessions that are quite common in the sports world and generally a lot of fun, this session was, to one woman according to her report, not much fun at all. What she said this baseball player did to her was to "grab her wrist and try to kiss her, then to pull her through a door."

The trouble is with most of these reports in newspapers around the country, that is today's news. And, I guess we have to admit, it is somewhat mild "news" although not very important. Tomorrow's newspaper will have new news, maybe even about another "celebrity," who has been charged with going "too far" with one or more women.

In this case, the player, and his team might help, will probably just settle by paying her to drop the matter. Guilty or not, this is often the usual result in these situations. Or, less likely, he might fight. What he did say, according to the newspaper, was "I deeply sympathize with anyone who has experienced sexual harassment. There is no place for it in our society."

That is pretty much what most of us men would say under these circumstances. Maybe he was just "kidding around," and did go too far, or maybe he wanted to rape her right there in front of everyone.

In fact there is more to this story which could indicate that he might not be the total brute she claims him to be. The photographer also said to a newspaper that about a half hour later, the player, the photographer, and some others, left the mall where the first photo session was being held, to "visit another store." She said she went along with the group in order to "not create a scene." To most of us, an "attempted rape" or a "plan to rape" or an "indication that a rape is coming" or anything else remotely like this, is far more than simply "creating a scene."

It is very close to a crime.

Meanwhile, either at the first store, or at the second store (the newspaper didn't go into these details) he again tried flirting with her, then tried to kiss her, then he tried to pull her through another door as he was seeking a restroom. She said he "made me go with him" to the second mall even though she said she was "screaming" and didn't want to go.

Where the police were during all of this apparent commotion that she said included "screaming" is not yet known, but may come out in court in the future.

After a "solid ten minutes of fighting," she said, he finally gave up. The newspapers, perhaps aware that this is a rather small bit of news in a society where everyone seems to be assaulting everyone, or at least where men seem to be assaulting women regularly, that could be that.

Her final quote in the newspaper, before this just joins the flood of complaints about "sexual harassment" in the past few months, was "Every time I have to hear about how great people think he is, I'm reminded of how awful he actually is and how he hurt me."

Yeah, he's a brute, without a doubt. Or at least, if we assume this woman, and all of the others, are telling the absolute truth. But what if they are stretching some points, or downright lying, or seeking publicity for themselves?

And if you think this baseball player is a bum, consider Harvey Weinstein, a producer who has been accused during this same time period of various forms of sexual misbehavior ranging from harassment to rape, and by up to *eighty* various women. Remember the word "accused" please. Although in Weinstien's case it does look pretty convincing.

Weinstein has been fired from his company and kicked out of the movie academy, and has been the focus, according to the Los Angles Times in their December 30, New Year's Eve morning edition, of several criminal investigations and lawsuits. Weinstein, and quite a large number of other men, were featured, with their photos, in an LA Times double page story about men who have been accused of harassing women sexually in some way or other.

Weinstein, and most of the others, has categorically denied everything. He has insisted that he has never assaulted a woman, and that he has never participated in non-consensual sex. To get to the bottom line, it is very true that he was, until all of these lawsuits hit, in an extremely powerful position. He could say "jump" and everybody around him would jump as high as they could. And he could get a young actress in a choice role in a film by just pointing his finger at the producer and nodding all the way across the set. Weinstein was the epitome of Hollywood power.

But come on now, let's get real about this. How could eighty women be lying about one person, or even just stretching the truth about something as personal as sexual harassment?

"He grabbed me by the hair and forced me to do something I did not want to do. He then dragged me to the bathroom and forcibly raped me," said one "Italian model-actress" who, according to the Times, said this happened in 2003, and according to the Times story, it happened in a hotel room. Yeah, you could ask why they were in a hotel room, and maybe even why he didn't "drag" her to the bed instead of the bathroom, but that may all come out in dozens of court actions, since in America, we aren't supposed to "rush to judgment" on any case.

Everyone, including Harvey Weinstein, is, in this country, innocent until proven guilty, and, in this country, must be given the opportunity to "be heard."

This might be especially true in cases that could be settled out of court between an "Italian model-actress" and a very, very rich man. There have been many other cases as 2017 drew to a close, and 2018 opened its doors to more cases of sexual harassment.

The page in the LA Times that discussed this unpleasant subject listed Weinstein and fifteen other men, with caricatured and quite unflattering images in a two-page hard-hitting spread that was apparently factual, contained many quotes from women, included mostly men in the entertainment business, and also included excellent actor Kevin Spacy, who was accused making a sexual advance by actor Anthony Rapp.

The author, who is straight, has tried to imagine how one gay man approaches another, thinking that the other is gay, but what do you say to suggest a friendship? Of more importance, perhaps, is the fact that several other men quickly came forward and said that Spacey had also approached them. Meanwhile, Spacey has apologized for whatever they think he did wrong, and closed the matter by stating, "I choose now to live as a gay man." Some of his accusers insist that he "assaulted" them, but in the real world where we have courts of law, one person is not even permitted, in the legal sense, to touch another person, even to patting them on the shoulder, without the possibility of a lawsuit. Lawyers, who make a ton of money in these matters, know that it is true that "Anyone can sue anyone," and they could add, "for anything."

Meanwhile, Spacy was dropped from the television series "House of Cards" and replaced in screen writer David Scarpa's "All the Money in the World." And everyone *seemed* to understand why. Without a question of a doubt, Spacy was guilty as charged, at least in the eyes of the media, and *must* be made to pay.

Hold on! Not really *everyone*, upon second thought. Some of us still think that some of these things are private, and until someone is really hurt, should remain private. If you are a woman or a man, and you are brutally raped, you must act. A crime has been committed, and the criminal must pay.

But if a casual friend, or anyone else for that matter, slaps you on the back in friendship, taking them to court on an assault charge doesn't seem right to many of us.

The LA Times may have made one real mistake when they printed a full page cartoon ad by someone named "Horsey" that suggested the latest motion picture from Hollywood was "Twilight of the Creeps," produced by "#MeToo Productions," and "starring" every one of the well-known men in show business now being accused of sexual misconduct. Misconduct by men of women, or by women of men, is not the slightest bit amusing. It is using power that you should not have against an opposite sex that is probably desperate and willing to do whatever you order them to do to receive what could be an otherwise very deserved favor that your power can arrange. There is nothing funny about it, and a newspaper of the stature of the Times should know this. This page in question is not funny and the editor, in my opinion, was wrong to approve it. There is a problem in the country today, and Spacey and Weinstein and many others are certainly involved, but to most of us, none of this is at all funny.

The paper, and the cartoon by Horsey, also included in the bottom right a caricature of a man in a bathrobe that appears perhaps to be a very rough sketch of Hugh Hefner. Many feel strongly that the creator and longtime boss of "Playboy Magazine" did an excellent job of introducing America to humorous, lightly clad women enjoying sexual freedom. And in a magazine where you had to spend several bucks for one issue, or simply couldn't afford to read it (there was no convenient Internet back then). So many Americans didn't buy, or read, Playboy. But the magazine, due to Hefner's drive and ambition and ability to see ahead, made "Hef," quite wealthy along the way, and until his passing he certainly seemed to be enjoying it all in his "mansion" in Los Angeles.

Unless "artist" Horsey was attempting to depict someone other than Hefner in the work he did for the Times, and missed the mark? That is possible, of course, and in that case the author apologizes with a request that Horsey be more precise with his drawings.

While all this was going on, most of the citizens of Great Britain were exerting mounting pressure on authorities who had approved the release of a taxi driver accused and convicted of assaulting dozens of women in his cab. He had spent less than ten years behind bars, and many felt that wasn't near enough time served for what he did.

Cabbie James Worboys had been convicted in 2009 of raping or sexually assaulting twelve women he had picked up in his cab as passengers. His plan was simple. He would tell his victims that he won a large amount of money in the lottery, and that he would like them to join him in a drink just to celebrate his good luck. The drink, however, was laced with a "knock out drop" and he would then rape them while they were unconscious. Of the one hundred two women who alleged that he had raped them, ten came forward to testify, and most of them were assured that Worboys would spend many years in prison after his almost certain conviction.

Britain's Parole Board said that a "panel" had approved the release of Worboys, and that they were forbidden to discuss the matter further. They also refused to say whether the victims had been consulted. However, Yvonne Traynor, chief executive of Rape Crisis South London, did say that Worboys had served a "woefully short time in prison," for what he had done. And Kim Harrison, of the Slater Gordon law firm in London, the firm that represented several of the victims, told BBC that the women felt "betrayed and devastated."

Even prominent hospitals are now being investigated for keeping rape a secret. The Cleveland Clinic, one of the nation's most renowned hospitals, admits to knowing of at least two doctors who were accused of raping patients and still kept them on the staff while reaching a "confidential settlement," with the victims, according to a USA Today investigation. Both doctors have left Cleveland Clinic for other hospitals. But Kristin Fehr, one of the women who claims she was raped by a colorectal surgeon while she was sedated during a procedure, has gone forward with the case, which she claims was expunged so the doctor could keep his license to practice.

Chapter Seven

Sexual Misconduct is described on the Internet by the University of Iowa, and many other such learned places, as being a "broad term encompassing any unwelcome behavior of a sexual nature that is committed without consent or by force, intimidation, coercion, or manipulation. Sexual misconduct can be committed by a person of any gender, and it can occur between people of the same or different genders.

Examples of sexual misconduct may vary in its severity and consists of a range of behavior or attempted behavior. It can occur between strangers or acquaintances, including people involved in an intimate or sexual relationship."

"Sexual misconduct includes, but is not limited to, the following examples of prohibited conduct as sexual assault, sexual harassment, sexual exploitation, and sexual intimidation."

Then, often following, is a definition of "consent."

"Consent is a freely and affirmatively communicated willingness to participate in particular sexual activity or behavior, expressed either by words or clear, unambiguous actions. It is the responsibility of the person who wants to engage in the sexual activity to ensure that consent is obtained from the other person to engage in the activity."

"Sexual assault," according to the same university, is "misconduct and represents a continuum of conduct from forcible intercourse to nonphysical forms of pressure that compel individuals to engage in sexual activity against their will. Examples of sexual assault under this policy include, but are not limited to, the following behaviors, however slight, when consent is not present. Sexual intercourse (anal, oral, or vaginal). Intercourse, however slight, meaning vaginal penetration by a penis, object, tongue, or finger; anal penetration by a penis, object, tongue, or finger; or oral copulation (mouth to genital contact or genital to mouth contact), including attempted sexual intercourse (anal, oral, or vaginal); intentional contact with the breasts, buttocks, groin, or genitals, or touching another with any of these body parts, or making another touch you or themselves with or on any of these body parts; any other intentional unwanted bodily contact of a sexual nature; use of coercion, manipulation, or force to make someone else engage in sexual touching, including breasts, chest, and buttocks."

That really covers it, for sure, and doesn't leave much room for argument for a court of law.

"Sexual harassment," once again from the Internet of the University of Iowa, "is a form of discrimination that includes verbal, written, or physical behavior of a sexual nature, directed at an individual, or against a particular group, because of that person's or group's gender, or based on gender stereotypes or manifestation, when that behavior is unwelcome and meets either of the following criteria:

"Submission or consent to the behavior is believed to carry consequences for another person's education, employment, on-campus living environment, or participation in a University program or activity. Examples of this type of sexual harassment include: pressuring a student to engage in sexual behavior for some educational or employment benefit; or making a real or perceived threat that rejecting sexual behavior will carry a negative consequence for the student in education, on-campus residence, or University program or activity.

"The behavior has the effect of limiting or denying another person's work or educational performance or creating an intimidating, hostile, or demeaning environment for employment, education, on-campus living, or participation in a University program or activity. Examples of this type of sexual harassment can include: persistent unwelcomed efforts to develop a romantic or sexual relationship; unwelcome commentary about an individual's body or sexual activities; repeated unwanted sexual attention; repeated and unwelcome sexually oriented teasing, joking, or flirting; verbal abuse of a sexual nature.

"Comments or communications could be verbal, written, or electronic. Behavior does not need to be directed at or to a specific student, but rather may be generalized unwelcomed and unnecessary comments based on sex or gender stereotypes. Determination of whether alleged conduct constitutes sexual harassment requires consideration of all the circumstances, including the context in which the alleged incidents occurred.

"Sexual exploitation," according to the same University, "involves taking nonconsensual, unjust, or abusive sexual advantage of another person. Examples can include, but are not limited to the following behaviors: electronically recording, photographing, or transmitting intimate or sexual utterances, sounds, or images without the knowledge and consent of all parties involved; voyeurism (spying on others who are in intimate or sexual situations); distributing intimate or sexual information about another person without that person's consent; prostituting or trafficking another person.

Finally, "Sexual intimidation" is defined, at least in Iowa, and who can argue with a state that is the "River City" setting for the wonderful "Music Man" musical by Meredith Willson, "involves: threatening another person that you will commit a sex act against them; or engaging in indecent exposure. Most of these crimes, and they are crimes, have been committed, according to the accusers, against them by the growing number of men they have accused, and possibly hope to meet them in court, or be paid off to drop the entire matter."

Chapter Eight

There is a fine and quite gigantic seventeen foot long painting done by French artist Jacques-Louis David back in 1799 that illustrated the power of women. It is in the Louvre Museum in Paris, France, and is called "The Intervention of the Sabine Women." The huge painting depicted naked and nearly naked women, some carrying children and all running directly between two fighting armies to stop a war they hate, one that is killing their men. The women are being pushed around by naked and near naked warriors who are no doubt quite surprised to see naked women on the battlefield. One woman is holding a baby high as if to keep the poor little kid from harm. But even back then, when women get irritated enough to take action, they take ACTION! The painting is meant, according to the experts, to be an example of women's power, although in David's picture, the women appear to be in real trouble. But the war does end, and that is all the women were trying to accomplish. How can you possibly fight a battle with spears and swords with very attractive naked women running around getting in the way?

Women today do have yet another brand new power over men, and they don't have to run between fighting armies to exert this power. It seems at first glance that a woman, or especially a group of women, need only say that a man, especially a well known man, has done something they consider sexually unpleasant or prohibited in the last week or month or year or dozens of years. The power is called "lawsuit." Why are today's women doing this?

Perhaps the women want the man punished in some way, either jail, which some of the men may well deserve, or at least a "pay off" of some kind, probably in cold cash. The original Sabine women in the painting only wanted to stop a war, and according to historians, they did. So naturally Broadway in New York City jumped on the idea, and a show resulted called "Seven Brides for Seven Brothers." It was a big, successful, musical show, and if you listen carefully, you'll hear a song called "Sobbin' Women." That gives you a hint that once again women may be in charge. But men also seem to enjoy this show completely.

The show was a smash hit on Broadway, and everywhere else it has been staged. They even made a great motion picture on this great plot.

"Seven Brides" was produced on stage at the Cabrillo Music Theater in Thousand Oaks, California, a year or so ago and once again audiences loved it. It is a show that has been produced over the past few years in many theaters around the United States. It even appears in some high school "Senior Class Plays" across the country. If have a chance to see this production done by a reasonable group of performers, note that once again women are generally in charge. Even when they are being kidnapped and hauled up a mountain. The truth is, even screaming women can only appear to be terrified, and the beauty is, the audience knows it.

The Thousand Oaks show, done by top professional singers and dancers, was a big local hit, and offered "standing room only" to local theater lovers. It was called by the same name, "Seven Brides for Seven Brothers," as it was on Broadway, and is based all the way back to artist David's "Intervention" and even further back to Nicolas Poussin's 1634 "Rape of the Sabine Women." The details of both paintings are fascinating. Online the painting is quite vivid, and the word "Rape" is either agreed to or fought as being misused by experts, exactly like this book may be debated a couple of hundred years from now, assuming my faithful readers are still buying it.

"Seven Brides" is a wonderfully entertaining show about a close family of men who live high up on a mountain and a group of unmarried women who live in a village at the bottom of the mountain.

It could even remind you of Mary Beard's best selling book "Women in Power." In her book, Beard discusses the power of women that was envisioned by Jacques-Louis David, back in 1799 in his "Intervention" painting, and by Poussin even earlier, in 1634, with his "Rape" painting.

The excellent Thousand Oaks, California, "Cabrillo" production, involved the family of men high in the mountains, and the women down below. You know from the beginning, of course, that these two groups are going to get together, but that knowledge doesn't make this show any less fun or entertaining. The film of the same name they made is just as entertaining. In fact, you hope for this happy conclusion throughout, while the audience of each production gets to witness marvelous dancing (including an almost unbelievable "challenge dance," where a dancer might be thrown high into the air by other dancers to a place on the stage where there is no one to catch her, and then, suddenly, a "catcher" appears just in the nick of time) and a very realistic, thundering avalanche on stage that is a part of the plot, and separates the ones up above from the ones down below in a very unique way.

The point of this is that even back a hundred or so years ago, men and women were in combat with each other, with each side hoping that it would all work out.

Almost every man interviewed for this book said he would absolutely not like to be a woman, although there were exceptions. And almost every woman, in spite of what we men think about "having babies" or "penis envy" and such, are quite happy being women, and would not want to change even if change was possible, as it now is in some cases. This is the conclusion from a rather extensive survey conducted over many months by the author.

Men like being men, and women like being women, as a very general rule. If you are not surprised, you are a part of the vast majority of men and women.

Then along comes famed Olympic champion Bruce Jenner, and it all goes out the window. Those who knew Bruce before his gender change, including the author of this book (who co-wrote a book with Bruce and his quite lovely first wife) had always found him, as did the author, to be masculine, a man who thoroughly enjoyed all the "boy toys" he had since he was a very celebrated Olympic champion, and toy companies and motorcycle companies and many other companies wanted him to be seen and photographed with their product. Most of Bruce's acquaintances were quite surprised, even shocked, at how it all turned out with Bruce.

Jenner had also seemed to casual friends to have a warm and pleasant relationship with his first wife, a lovely, very attractive woman. There never seemed to be a trace, at least among those who knew him as casually as the author knew him, that he wished for a change of gender. But almost every one of them who knew him, once again including the author, are now totally supportive of her, and will argue that Caitlyn Jenner can do with her life as she pleases, as we can all do with our lives. She is a lovely woman now, and it is none of our business what she had to go through to be a woman.

But this doesn't happen often, although it is quite possible in this day and age. An Olympic champion, as Jenner was, must live through the publicity of such a change, but otherwise it is his, or her, right to change gender, knowing that eventually the publicity will die down and life will go on. In the Broadway show about Seven Brides, everyone seemed happy to be what they were, but it didn't seem possible that the fourteen could work things out and be together finally as couples. One group of seven, remember, lived high in the mountains, the other group of seven lived far down below. The men, in one scene, desperately wanted the women, and in another the women wanted the men, but isn't that the way it really is?

And would we really want to change it?

But then, getting back to the Sabine women plot, the mountain men just decided to ride into town, pick up the girls from wherever they were casually hiding, and carry them back up the mountain to their new home. Talk about the power of women, they certainly had power in this show. This is what the Roman army did centuries ago to the women of Sabine, according to the leader of the men in the mountains, the one who could read. And he had read a book about what the Romans did to the Sabine women. So he instructed his brothers on what they *should* do, to get wives. He already had a wife he had picked up down below. Of course it wasn't legal then, and it isn't legal now. Women and men must agree before they make drastic moves, like getting married, or even engaged.

One of the beauties of this show is that the girls didn't really mind what is happening all that much, and the audience knows it. Oh, they may protest very mildly, but they know what's going on. The girls knew the men casually, as the more "polished" folks in the village knew their rough-shod neighbors up on the mountain, and the men knew the women as neighbors. Most of the pairs, fortunately, had even become "couples" in mind if not in body, so that does smooth things out a little and makes one of the shows hit songs, a mournful "Make It Through the Winter," more logical and understandable. But I think we can all agree that what the seven brothers of the "Pontipee" family did in their mass kidnapping was very wrong, just as the Roman army was wrong centuries ago, and just as modern men are wrong who force themselves on modern women.

In fact, let's be absolutely honest. Also just as many modern women, actresses and models and others not in show business, have possibly been wronged. We don't know that yet, but it does seem logical. Some of the "wronged women" will be paid off in money, and some will go to the courts, and then there will be more conclusions in any sequel to this book.

But, because of the avalanche (that is amazing to see onstage) the Pontipee brothers are stuck with a very long winter up there in the cold mountains of Oregon. The woman in charge of the girls, the happy wife of the leader of the Pontipee boys, continues to be as strict as possible. She is absolutely in charge, and she is a "good" woman. This includes insisting that that both the Pontipee boys and the town girls, although hungry to be together through the long cold winter, must sleep apart. Boys sleep in the barn and girls sleep in the house, and absolutely no exceptions are permitted although some of the couples do try. And since the avalanche prevented anyone authorized to marry to make it up the mountain to where the Pontipee boys and the town girls are living, none of the couples, according to the woman in charge, could properly finalize their relationship with a minister before they…well…you know.

It is a lovely show with a fine conclusion, and leaves no doubt that women are in charge, sometimes eventually, as it could be in our modern life, but almost always one way or the other.

It all seemed to have been started when fine TV and motion picture actor Bill Cosby was said to have taken advantage of a number of women, and as the story grew, mountains of publicity followed. Did he or did he not drug some of these women into unconsciousness and then use them for sex?

Surely not fan favorite Bill Cosby. Bill, an all time favorite on TV, would never do such a bad thing. Drug women and then rape them?

Not possible! Yet the story remains. It is plowing through the court system at the writing of this book at a snail's pace, and the several actions against Cosby have not yet been heard in open court, and by the accusers. In fact, there are a flood of complaints from other women against other men occurring today, the women insisting they have been used in one way or another by men they have named, and with most of the men denying it. The Los Angeles District Attorney, according to a story in the Los Angeles Times, is "reviewing" two specific sex crimes filed by "prominent actresses" against one of the men involved. This case was presented to them by Beverly Hills police detectives. But all told, the D.A. is said to be reviewing an amazing several *hundred* such cases. But the days of picking up a woman in a bar for some quick sex seem to be gone forever. While the DA of LA is reviewing cases against many, many men, and somewhere, although it doesn't for some reason appear to be nearly as interesting, there may be an occasional "man against woman" among these cases, the courts grind on.

Fine actor and race car driver Paul Newman openly approaches lovely Charlotte Rampling in a bar in the film "The Verdict." He picks her up, takes her to his home, and almost immediately begins to kiss her. They both know what is going to happen, and they both seem to look forward to it. Those were the "good old days" for guys who hang around bars, as Newman is very well portraying.

Chapter Nine

Everyone seems to be paying attention, or at least is being affected by, the new rush to judgment involving men who have been accused of going too far with a women. Back in the old days, a man could "kid" with a woman, but now this can be "going too far." Please consider once again my issue with the department store lady. I wanted to buy something, she wanted to sell it, but she leaned over too close during the negotiations. Her breast was within inches of my hand there on the counter. We kidded about it, we were friendly about it, but she moved her breast back just enough, and thanked me. And then, as I said before, she was probably quite happy to watch me walk away.

In the old days a man could even meet a woman in a bar, give her a hug, buy her a drink, and take her home for the night. Who among us more senior men have not done that? In fact, who among somewhat more senior women have not done the same? Now, that could be very risky for both genders, since almost certainly sex is the objective. The trouble is, the man or woman who was given the free drink could roar back tomorrow with a policeman and insist that the man raped her.

"Then why did you go home with him in the first place?" the policeman might ask.

"Because he forced me to go home with him," she might answer.

"How did he force you?" the policeman might respond. "Did you scream in protest as he hurried you out of the bar?"

"No, I didn't want to make a scene."

"A scene is what you really needed," the cop might say,

"But he said he would murder my children if I didn't go home with him and give him what he wanted."

"Why didn't you shout or scream?"

"Just because I...well...didn't want to make a scene," is actually one of the answers police get.

So the man is hauled off to jail pretty much without further consideration. And jail is where perhaps he should be, and he might even be abused by the other inmates. Which he may richly deserve.

It is even possible, although probably not very likely, that Harvey Weinstein is totally innocent, as innocent as a new born baby, and until that case against him, and the cases against all the other men now being accused, are settled, this is still America, where you must be proven guilty before we should accept that you are guilty. And even the courts make mistakes there, too.

And the court will rule. Who saw and heard what during the evening? And which witness who was sober and can remember can be trusted to give a logical story as the lawyers, and none of them are working "pro bono," try to form their case. Did the two walk out together, or did he drag her? Was she screaming "I'm being raped!" as she is now doing?

Did she fight back?

Even the women in Playboy Magazine, and some models are now claiming that they were being "used," always back then said they chose to be photographed, and enjoyed being photographed, and certainly wanted to be featured in the racy magazine. The author of this book was careful interviewing, fully clothed of course (both the author and the model), one of the "Penthouse" stark naked models (this expensive magazine was a competitor of Playboy a few years ago) and this magazine exhibited even *more revealing* naked ladies. There was no part of the human female body that Penthouse wouldn't, and didn't, feature, and that included everything. It thundered into intense competition with Hefner's magazine.

The very pretty young nude model interviewed by the author said the same thing. The publicity quite revealing photos in Penthouse Magazine brought to her as a model, and the pay she received, made it all worthwhile. And she knew exactly what she would say to her children in a few years, and that was that she loved posing in the nude, and that she would do it again anytime as a "nude model" being paid for her work. That is exactly what beautiful actress Marilyn Monroe often said, and she was a marvelous success.

And, *WOW*, was the interview session with the Penthouse model ever revealing in Penthouse Magazine. The author naturally had to study the photos in order to do a good interview. Which once again indicates the power of women over men.

Penthouse is long gone now, and so is Playboy planning soon to be "long gone," and since no competitors have started up, maybe they are both gone forever.

Playboy has even officially announced that they will probably very soon cease publication. The magazine recently stopped using photos of nude women and will (although it was photos of nude women who rocketed the magazine to one of the most popular of all) according to the ones in charge now that Hugh Hefner is gone, change into being a "brand management company" rather than a company who publishes a famous magazine. The magazine has dropped from twelve issues every year to six, and they no longer feature completely nude ladies at all. Perhaps Hefner was right back when he started. But eventually circulation of Playboy dropped from several million to about five hundred thousand per month, which is another sign that says there will be no competitors until some editor with the courage and know-how of "Hef" shows up to open a new magazine.

There is even one man now publicly insisting that what is happening is "reverse discrimination against men." He said he has been banned from Alaska Airlines for "touching the buttocks of a female flight attendant" during an evening flight. He says he only wanted to order a drink, and was only trying to get her attention. He says he only touched her lower back.

So he was escorted from the airplane by a policeman and has been banned from further flights on Alaska Airlines.

"For me to be accused of this, and for me to be escorted off the plane by a policeman?" he complained to reporters. "This is it. I'm blowing up. It's unnecessary. It's discrimination toward me," he said. Many men agree with him.

According to the L.A.Times, Alaska Airlines is developing and updating policies and training "to ensure that crew members have the tools they need to prevent, identify and address sexual harassment on board, and will have more to say about what that looks like later this winter."

Was this man treated fairly, or not? Many noted men are losing the respect of millions, while this man lost only his right to fly on one airline. But it isn't over yet. Watch for the outcome in the newspapers as the gears of the courts grind slowly forward, especially on the West Coast, where Alaska Airlines and the entertainment business are best known.

It does seem that by the end of 2017, many of us, men and women, were aware of all that is happening, and are in our own minds "developing and updating" our thoughts about it all. But most of us, and most men, certainly, are in a place where the obvious logical conclusions all have loopholes. Dozens of women are swearing out warrants for men who appear very guilty, but may not be guilty at all. Remember the author's situation with my co-host on the TV show? Although everything, including the damning photo (which perhaps would not be permitted as evidence in any court action since it was not legally taken), pointed to my guilt. I was as innocent as a new born baby. I was only trying to help a fellow worker, and I did succeed, even to her own very adult, very sweet acknowledgement.

Chapter Ten

Recently "hundreds" of women, three hundred according to the newspapers and including well-known actresses Reese Witherspoon and Shonda Rimes, did launch an initiative to combat sexual harassment in Hollywood. They call their action "Times Up" and announced details about the new organization in a full page ad in the New York Times and on every social media they can reach.

The initiative is said to include a legal defense fund to help women protect themselves from sexual misconduct, and also to penalize negligent companies (who, presumably don't agree with them) and finally to cut the use of nondisclosure agreements (which can open the door to problems). What the group also wants is gender parity at Hollywood studios and talent agencies, and what they have requested is for women walking the red carpet at the annual Golden Globes celebration, and other such productions, to wear black.

They apparently haven't yet put out any suggestions about men who have been molested in some way, and need help with the expenses of lawyers and courts. But men usually wear black tuxedoes to that function anyhow.

That remains to be seen each year from now on, but almost certainly Rimes and Witherspoon arrived dressed in black, and so did many other celebrity actors and show business folks. From bright red outfits, black was the way. And "parity" doesn't seem unreasonable, even to most men.

In the group's letter to the Times, they stated, "To every woman employed in agriculture who has had to fend off unwanted sexual advances from her boss, every housekeeper who has tried to escape an assaultive guest, every janitor trapped nightly in a building with a predatory supervisor, every waitress grabbed by a customer and expected to take it with a smile, every garment and factory worker forced to trade sexual acts for more shifts, every domestic worker or home health aide forcibly touched by a client, every immigrant woman silenced by the threat of her undocumented status being reported in retaliation for speaking up and to women in every industry who are subjected to indignities and offensive behavior that they are expected to tolerate to make a living: We stand with you. We support you."

Who can argue with that?

And the "Times Up" strong group of organizers includes actresses, agents, writers, directors, producers and other entertainment executives, with actresses Ashley Judd, Eva Longoria, Emma Stone and Kerry Washington, and even Universal Pictures Chairwoman Donna Langley as well as Tina Tehen, who served as First Lady Michelle Obama's Chief of Staff, as members. The result of this powerful group of women? Did the Golden Globes ceremony show any change?

You *bet* it did.

The famous ceremony that is shown on television across the county and around the world, and which normally features the "red carpet" approach to the auditorium, was *blanketed* with *black.*

Most of the men were in their traditional black, but many of the women who normally attend and always show up in startling ensembles of bright colors and strange, often very revealing designs, were also in black. "Me Too" had a tremendous and profound effect on the Golden Globes, proving once again that women have the power to make unbelievable changes in our lives, in what we expect, in what we think. Who would have thought that pretty actresses who had planned all year to be "wearing Tom Ford" would show up at the Golden Globes in black.

But then we must consider the college football coach who recently had a female administrative assistant who accused him of sexual misconduct. Because of that, the coach was fired. Did you read that? Because of an *accusation*, he was fired. Even worse, he will probably end up in court accused of sexual harassment and who knows what else in an extremely expensive lawsuit against him. These things do seem to grow as the matter progresses, and the lawyers get involved. It is already over several million now, including the current suit against the coach, and climbing.

This coach's assistant filed the multimillion dollar claim accusing the coach of sexually harassing her and creating a very "hostile working environment."

This man was a respected coach with a good team from a good college, not at all like the assistant coach from one of the best football colleges in the nation who was convicted of ugly things with young boys he would take into the team's shower room. This latter coach was tried, convicted, and sent to prison, where he is now serving a long sentence.

This is different. This matter is a man against a woman, both adults, and a third woman who has become involved.

This married coach is accused of having an affair with another woman, and his assistant, who is the accuser, had to "cover" for him from time to time, even on the sidelines at football games. And even though she had worked for the school for several years, the accuser, who has filed a claim insisting that she felt "constant pressure" to "hide" the coach's extramarital affair from his wife, just simply "could take no more." She even claimed that others on the sports staff had to participate in the problems created by the coach's affair with the third woman. So she took action, and the action resulted in the firing of the coach by the college, who conducted the investigation.

Apparently, according to the college, the investigation only indicated that the "direction and climate" of the football program was wrong, and this is the basis for the firing of the coach. Meanwhile, the coach, who was "deeply disappointed" in the actions, continues to insist that his firing was wrong, and that any evidence against him of harassment was "baseless and false," and this could be true. He only admitted to the extra marital affair, and said he is trying to work things out with his wife. Now yet another of the expanding number of "sexual" cases must be added to await decisions by one court or another.

As usual, the findings of any court of the future will decide this case, or, more likely, it will be settled out of court, and meanwhile the swarm of such cases will continue. Certainly, though, many of them will be settled by a quiet "payoff" if the accused, man or woman, can afford it.

Today, though, there are very few women, if any, on the "accused" side of these legal actions. They are generally on the "accuser" side. True, it would be almost amusing to see a woman try to rape a man, so the lawsuits are almost universally against men so far.

And the author of this book, who flew combat missions in the Korean War, who is proud to be an American, and who loves this country, and who also supports President Trump in his very difficult job, feels we are heading in a questionable, or at least confused, direction, with this flood of lawsuits against men.

Many of whom almost certainly had no idea they were stepping "over the line," although some of them certainly did know they were going too far, or demanding too much. Maybe some of them were seriously "kidding around", or maybe even trying to get sex from a woman, and doing it quite obviously, but without a thought of rape, which is against the law.

Meanwhile. another newspaper said in the easy to read headline "ESPN fires McNabb, Davis, in a sex misconduct probe." A "probe," but not a conviction. Donovan McNabb and Eric Davis, who were employed by the NFL Network, (that's National Football League) worked for ESPN Radio, and were taken off the air December 12, 2017, "pending an investigation." Both men were former NFL players, and were among seven men named in a lawsuit against NFL Enterprises by a former NFL Network stylist, Jami Cantor. The lawsuit says McNabb sent Cantor "sexually explicit messages" during his time at NFL Network. Davis is accused in the suit only of "making lewd comments." How many men in the United States could swear to God that they have never in their life made a "lewd" comment to a woman? These things, I'm sorry to say, happen in an "easy-to-honestly-forget" moment, often to a lady you know pretty well, and are also very often said to be forgotten, or chuckled at, or perhaps even apologized for.

But to be brought into court, with lawyers, who are trying to prove that you are a "slime?"

Chaper Eleven

Let's lay it on the line where we can all see it. Suppose, just suppose, that one of the men, the one who sent "suggestive, sexually specific messages," sent a text message to the woman that said, "I really like you, I think you are beautiful, and I would love to sleep with you. Is that a possibility for us?"

Pretty suggestive, right? Even stepping "well over the line" most of us might agree, right? But worth a couple of million dollars, if the accused or his insurance company, can afford it? Think about that, because the man either knows the lady very well, or he is just "playing around," and where it shouldn't happen, it does happen.

The days of "playing around" are pretty much over, and both men and women are going to miss these more carefree days, or make a fortune on them. And eventually it can turn off any entire industry that hires both men and women who must, by job description, work together every day. There is a much quicker, easier way for a man to be satisfied by a woman he doesn't necessarily love, or even, perhaps, really respect. Or for a man and another man, depending on the men, or in fact for two women who enjoy such things. This way takes very little time with most participants, is more convenient for all involved, requires almost no undressing, leaves no after-sex signs to be analyzed, and is really much more convenient for all involved. Many of the lawsuits in the newspapers of today involve this method of attaining satisfaction, almost always by men with a woman.

It is called "oral sex," and occurs when a woman "goes down" on a man, or when a man goes down on a woman, or any other combination of men and women. In this procedure, if it is a woman pleasing a man, and is the most popular technique mentioned in modern lawsuits, the woman allows the man to get his enjoyment when she takes his "manhood" into her mouth, that's the "oral" part, then she moves in up and down ways soon causing him to have an orgasm.

This is quick and easy, and quite satisfying for the man, although not very much for most woman. It is an act of love between lovers, a "gift" a woman can give a man, or can even charge him a fee for the giving of the gift. This "oral sex" is quite often shown in modern pornographic films, always in full view, and the author had the pleasure of knowing, and even several times lunching with, the female "master" of this sex technique. Porn film actress Linda Lovelaces's one and only starring role in a widely viewed and very popular pornographic motion picture, shown only in X-Rated theaters or, after it was recorded, in private sessions, was called "Deep Throat."

This film that became a best seller, featured the oral sex expert of the ages, Linda, herself. Lovelace, a very nice and very pretty woman now gone, had a pleasant, outgoing personality, and a genuine, warm sense of humor when you got to know her.

As the author did.

We met while I was conducting the "Round Table" at the Greater Los Angeles Press Club every Thursday afternoon. I had asked Miss Lovelace to speak at a luncheon where one hundred or so reporters would, after lunch, fire questions at the scheduled guest speaker. I served as the Master of Ceremonies, and always sat next to the guest speaker. Linda, and any other guest from any field of endeavor, usually jumped at the chance to speak at the Greater Los Angeles Press Club because of the publicity that would follow, and so I met and dined with dozens of Governors and Senators and actors like Charlton Heston and actresses all the way up to Jane Fonda, right after her return from Viet

Nam. Charlton, also now gone, was great, but Jane was a tough one. I had permitted some unknown guests in the house to fill one long table for twelve. Each one at that table was a recently released, thin, gaunt, poorly uniformed prisoner of war from Viet Nam. It was a lunch meeting that brought all the big newspapers and TV stations to the LA Press Club, and solid publicity after lunch for the club, and for Jane Fonda and the other weekly speakers, although Jane didn't really need it.

I especially liked Linda Lovelace, and soon forgot her checkered history and "Deep Throat" appearances in our conversations. Nearby tables at our lunches in this Hollywood atmosphere paid plenty of attention to Linda, however. Seems like everyone in the room recognized her, even some folks I would have guessed had never seen "Deep Throat," or, for that matter, cared to see it.

This was true at the first lunch and at several other lunches we arranged just because Linda and I seemed to "get along" with each other. She was an intelligent woman with a strange sexual "skill," and you would have to see the movie if you haven't figured out yet what that skill was. It is probably still available on the "restricted" shelves where they sell "X-rated" DVR's.

Please permit me one quick "aside," having to do with this program in my life. My very first cell phone call, and I'm a little proud of it, was from "Star Trek's" Leonard Nimoy, better known as "Mr. Spock." I treasure my friendship with Leonard, which began when he called from his car on his brand new "cell phone," to say he might be a moment or two late to a meeting. This was a long time ago, but it is still fresh in my memory. I apologize for boring you with it, but that friendship was important to me, and I am writing this book.

Linda Lovelace was a master at oral sex is the point of all this that I'm trying to make, not that I ever received this skill of hers. We seemed always to be surrounded by people who knew her. We were friends, and her skill was her business, and that was fine with me. And I miss our luncheon meetings.

But even generally distributed films often suggest, or even show, oral sex, probably between a man and a woman in love. There is a very entertaining, quite exciting film called "The Cooler" starring well-known actors William H. Macy, Alec Baldwin and Maria Bell, that is in general release, with warnings about some of the scenes. In the film,

Macy enjoys this very well acted oral sexual act from his co-star, lovely actress Maria Bell, who in the movie is very sweet, and very innocent, and anxious to please her man.

There is no doubt about what is happening between the two, but extremely visual views go to, and then just beyond, his orgasm. Still, if you want to see very pretty Miss Bell in her unbelievably scanty underwear, be sure to enjoy this film the next time it is on television. It may even be further "edited" for the more conservative members of the audience, but it is still very enjoyable, and quite exciting, especially as it nears the end.

Critics have said this is the "real" Las Vegas as being depicted by actor Baldwin as the boss of a casino trying to make a profit, with drugs and murders and brutal beatings included, and that is possible. All of these things take place "behind" the glitter and glamour of "The Las Vegas Strip."

The "sex scenes" in this movie, and there are several, are really quite charming. It is a fun movie about two folks, a man and a woman, who love each other in spite of many problems, and it has an ending that will really startle viewers. But how can an act that is often a "crime" be so openly shown in a modern motion picture distributed on the market, one that can be seen even by children? It can be released because of the careful but fun way the sex acts are handled, and because it is always a very legal expression of love between a man and a woman. But you will have to answer some possibly embarrassing questions from your kids, if you allow them to see this complex, often depressing but otherwise entertaining motion picture. Which the author advises against, where kids are concerned.

This is not the case with the flood of complaints from women who have been forced to perform the intimate act by men who could be more interested in power than in sex. Generally speaking and at the bottom line, since men and women have been on earth, when a woman is doing something sexual for a man like this, forced or not, it is for his pleasure, not for her pleasure. A woman who loves a man knows this, and can even enjoy giving this pleasure to her lover, but that is about all she gets unless the owner of the "wife store" back in the early part of this book can honestly add yet another intriguing line in the instructions for his second floor.

There is a very hard-hitting scene in the motion picture "The Shawshank Redemption" having to do with oral sex where the hero is on the verge of being forced to perform the act on another very "prison-powerful" convict. The lead actor in this film that won many major awards including an "Oscar," Tim Robbins, has already been badly beaten and the forced sex act is next. But the hero in this very hard-hitting film manages to convince the other convict, who has his group of supporters there to help him with whatever he wants, that the hero suffers from a "lock jaw" disease, and that once his jaw is closed, it cannot be forced open. And this is in a very serious scene in the film. It is not meant to be funny, and it certainly isn't even slightly amusing. If the powerful convict continues, he will be taking a chance on losing his penis. So the "bad guys" simply beat the weaker convict. Robbins, further, and then send him back to his cell. This is not a suggestion that the girls in these forced sexual situations should consider "biting down hard," but it sure cautioned this rather uneducated convict who, if he had gone to medical school and become a doctor, wouldn't have been "fooled." But there are very few medical doctors serving long term prison sentences.

Meanwhile, the 2017 annual statement from the University of California's "Annenberg Inclusion Initiative" once again does not speak very well concerning the number of women and minorities in positions of power in the entertainment business. There are women in Hollywood, directors and producers and actors, who have great power (so far, none of them seem to have been sued by lower ranking male co-workers), but generally the entertainment business is ruled by men. This attitude even grows and spreads, and the fact is, if you are seeking a role in an amateur play being staged by the local Lima, Ohio, drama group, it will probably be a man, not a woman, who offers you the part. Men are generally in charge wherever they go. But that, as it should, is gradually changing.

Women are catching up, and sometimes very quickly, it seems. Apparently the courts will have the opportunity to make many final decisions on the modern relationships between men and women.

Is it possible to "boil down" all that is happening? Will the Olympic boxer, now middle-aged, be permitted to teach kids, as he has been doing for years, about the fine art he has perfected and loves, or is that no longer going to be allowed for him?

Will the woman who said "I felt like a prostitute, an utter disappointment to myself, my parents, my friends. And I deserved not to tell anyone," as she spoke of an alleged encounter in a hotel room with a an important director who, she says, tried to "rub his crotch against her leg." be able to speak out? Or will she "never be cast in a film again?"

Will well known and quite talented actress Rose McGowan be able to prove it when she says, "All of you Hollywood 'A-list golden boys' are LIARS."

Another actress told the newspapers, "It's a career based on networking…not just what you know, but who you know. Speaking up could make it more difficult, if not impossible, to advance your own career," she said in a speech. Actress Silvia Castillo, describing an alleged encounter in the Los Angeles Times that she said she had with a California Assemblyman's Chief of Staff, said in 2010, "He grabbed me with one hand, grabbed my head and shoved his tongue into my mouth. With his other hand, he put it up my dress."

"What's really important right now is that there's an uprising…people are saying, 'No, this is problematic.' Women need to speak up, and women need to be heard," said actress Blake Lively in the same story in the Los Angeles Times. "It's not one industry, and it's every level of the food chain. It's just something women learn to write off as the day-to-day of being a woman; 'she asked for it because she wore a dress.' But thank God now the conversation is shifting."

There was an open letter circulated in Sacramento, California, that created a flood of letters from women from across the country. The letter also suggested that if one agrees, one should "sign" it by calling or writing.

The letter was entitled *"We Said Enough,"* although why these words were used is questionable since suddenly thousands of women seem to be thoroughly enjoying the outpouring of hate.

The open letter said the following.

"Each of us has endured, or witnessed, or worked with women who have experienced some form of dehumanizing behavior by men with power in our workplaces. Men have groped and touched us without our consent, made inappropriate comments about our bodies and our abilities."

That does open a whole flock of new doors, doesn't it? For example, it is a boss's job, and the boss is the one in power, to comment on the performance of an employee, up to and including firing that employee, man or woman, for not having the "ability" or the "strength of body" to do the job they were hired to do. This is just a little bit of "splitting hairs" in a way, but everybody seems to want to jump on the bandwagon. Hundreds of women in Sacramento, including elected officials, "signed" the "We Said Enough" statement.

Yet the author of this book has been around the country and around the world, often traveling with usually delightful and happy men and women. He travels and enjoys the company of these men and women, and yet without one single, solitary suggestion of "groping" or of any other "sexual misbehavior." Not a woman has complained when the author was in charge of a group of men and women about a single "sexual problem." It's always been an "if you don't like me, then I won't bother you" situation.

It does happen, of course, but for hundreds of women to sign on agreeing to the letter printed above is almost more like ladies wanting to be heard even if they haven't been touched or, rather, "groped.". It is possible that women are going too far now, and shouting too loudly about the mistreatment they claim to have suffered.

Chapter Twelve

Actor Liam Neeson seemed to hit things on the head in recent releases to newspapers that suggested we all need to slow down a little, and take some time to study what's going on, thinking about something before yelling about it.

Also, the woman who are speaking out are making some valuable points.

Maybe it has been available all along, but there is now a printed form that women can use when they feel they have been abused. It is ready and waiting, perhaps at every police station, where women can list the details.

And you didn't have to look very carefully to see the many female hosts, all female in fact, at the recent Screen Actors Guild awards. The previously discussed "Time's Up" claimed responsibility for the "all women" lineup. And the women hosts did a great job, too. But somehow, for some reason, it seems, men make better hosts and stand up comics. Overall, that is. There are certainly some dynamite women stand up comics, of course.

The author has been around show business people most of his life, especially since he moved to California. He likes show business folks. He enjoys their sense of humor, and hearing them talk about a movie he has seen, and hearing about sets he has been on. He has learned that some actors, and Ernest Borgnine jumps to mind, often responded to the "I love your work" comment with the question, "which movie are you speaking of?" Unless you really know the actor and his or her work, this can leave you speechless.

Not once, in all the times he has been around show business people, even back stage at the Oscars and Emmies and Grammies, where he has had a chance to chat with folks in the business, has the author ever witnesses a "grope." Not even with crowds around, and everyone pressing against everyone else, and major stars in the tight hallways between photo rooms, and even with autograph seekers restricted to the outside, there has never, in many years, been a single example of sexual harassment. It does happen, of course, but maybe two of the top actors in Hollywood, Liam Neeson and Clint Eastwood, both manly men who are probably very attractive to young women actresses, have views on the subject of harassment.

Meanwhile, gropes, and other such invasions, simply don't happen around most of these men. Why grope when all you really have to do is wink when you see an attractive woman?

"The Democrats thought I was going senile" back when he began to be in great demand as an actor, "and the Republicans were sure of it," said Eastwood.

"I finally became a Republican, but in the last few years, things have changed," he continued. "For example, I just say 'leave everyone alone when it comes to 'gay marriage.' There are so many more important things to talk about than gay marriage."

Neeson, who could without question have almost any one he wants for an intimate dinner, or a pleasant meeting, or even all night, and who could also thrill most young actresses by gently touching them, or for an all night meeting, (although the protesters will scream at those terrible suggestions) takes a softer view. And he also defends his friend, Dustin Hoffman, who has been accused of "inappropriate behavior" and "sexual misconduct" by a woman.

"There is a bit of a witch hunt happening," said Neeson about the recent deluge of sexual misconduct allegations against famous men. "There's some people, famous people, being suddenly accused of touching some girl's knee or something, and suddenly they're being dropped from their program." Now Liam Neeson is under fire for defending some famous men who have been accused.

Another well-known actor commented that "We seem to be mistaking seduction for harassment," which seems to hit the nail on the head to many men.

Neesen was specific in his defense of both Garrison Keillor and Dustin Hoffman. Keillor was fired from Minnesota Public Radio for "inappropriate behavior" and Hoffman has been accused of sexual misconduct by several women. Among them was actress Latjrum Rosetter, who alleged that Hoffman repeatedly groped her during their 1983 "Death of a Salesman" production on Broadway in New York. She didn't say during her interviews why she didn't just scream for help, but it was probably because she didn't want to "make a scene."

Both men are said to have "pushed back" against the allegations, and possibly even will fight it out in court.

Liam Neeson spoke out further, and opened yet another door. Actors seem to be even more superstitious than professional hockey goalies, who will often go to extremes to keep a "win streak" going. They will wear the same clothing, or skate onto the ice in a very strict line order with teammates, or move about in a certain way in or out of the goal crease before a game. Some actors are the same way, especially stage actors. When something is going well, *don't change it*, some actors feel.

"The Duston Hoffman thing, I'm on the fence about that," said Neeson. "Because when you're doing a play and you're with your family, other actors, technicians, you do silly things. You do silly things and it becomes kind of superstitious; if you don't do it every night, you think it's going to jinx the show. I think Duston Hoffman was…I'm not saying I've done similar things like what he did. Apparently he touched another girl's breast and stuff.

It's childhood stuff what he was doing."

But that does open the door to many possibilities, since actors and professional hockey goalies are certainly a breed all their own. You just happen to touch a fellow performer in an intimate way, and the show goes as smooth as glass that night, better than it has ever gone. Why not touch that same fellow actor in the same way again? What harm is there in that? You could even ask permission before the curtain goes up, just to be sure it's OK, but that, of course, could destroy the "mantra."

This has absolutely nothing to do with forcing one who is lower on the power list than you to give you oral sex. But Liam Neeson does make a point about superstitions, a point also having nothing at all to do with the countless women who will jump at the chance to lie down with a producer to get a role in his film. More power to them, for that matter. In an extremely competitive job in any field, a woman might do whatever it takes to break through any "glass ceiling." That is her business, not yours or mine.

Actor Liam Neeson says the current movement against men is not simply a

Hollywood action, it is in most industries. Appearing on the Irish talk show "The Late Late Show," Nesson said "There's some people, famous people, being suddenly accused of touching some girl's knee or something, and suddenly they're being dropped from their program or something."

Maybe that could be the final answer to everything, and that is to just "leave everyone alone."

"I don't care what they say," said Clint Eastwood, who has so far never been accused of going over the line by any beautiful actress, even though he has worked with dozens of them. He simply doesn't harass, and he also pays little attention to the whole sad situation. He minds his own business, as you might expect Clint Eastwood to do, and he doesn't seem to want to be involved. Maybe that's another answer. Men in wartime combat situations do not easily make friends with another man in their squad, or on their airplane in combat, because that person might be dead in a few minutes.

Don't do it, and don't get involved. That could handle it all.

Many feel that we are all moving too fast. A woman in any business should, of course, be respected. Neeson, one of my favorite actors but a man I have so far not yet had the pleasure of meeting, might have the best idea. He is in the business, he works around other show business folks, he does scenes with some of the most beautiful women in the world, and he seems to believe things are going too fast. Many men feel as he probably does, that there are too many "alleges" and "seems to be" and other such soft words being used.

There are very few "proof" words being used in this rush to judge many men. For instance, why doesn't some beautiful woman from show business, a woman who has faced the inequity herself, come forward and comment. Probably because her lawyer says "no comment."

One woman did, and boy did she *ever*? She is beautiful, she is outspoken, she was at the very top not that many years ago and still commands great respect, and she is still beautiful at the age of eighty three. She rose to fame in the fifties. She recently did an interview with Paris Match magazine. One of the first things she points out is that Hollywood actresses "have a long history of using their sexuality to advance their careers."

OK, so what? Most of us men know that. And what's so wrong with that? We'll need a little more before we insist upon throwing someone in jail for "allegedly" doing something that is a crime. This actress speaks out even more firmly. "The vast majority, although not women in general," she said to the magazine, "'come on' to producers, 'and then, so they'll be talked about, they say they were harassed."

She says, on the other hand, that she found it "charming" when men complimented her on her physique. "I thought it was nice to be told that I was beautiful" or even that I had a "nice rear end."

All of this, and more, came from sixties sex symbol Brigitte Bardot. She has openly said she thinks the growing "#MeToo movement" is "hyrocritical" and even "ridiculous." She said she has never been sexually harassed, and points out that the movement detracts from "important themes that could be discussed."

"In reality, rather than helping them, it hurts them," she said of the women who are dressing in black or charging forward on slim evidence, or demanding money from men they say harassed them. Bardot, long retired but still remembered for posing in the nude, is now a devoted and very well known animal rights activist.

From the teenager in Irvine, California, who was reported by the Associated Press in 2018 to have made a habit of streaking past female joggers and reaching out from his skateboard and patting them on the rear, to the Hollywood producers who have made a habit of demanding sex from struggling young female actors, the entire matter is still being watched over by women's groups and lawyers. And also by gay groups, who don't seem to want to be left out of the turmoil.

Times have changed. The days of "playing around" between sexes is long gone, and that is sad. From now on, and especially we men, must all be very careful what we say, and we must ask permission before we touch. Breasts and fannies are from now on pretty much off limits unless you are married, and even then you must be careful. He or she might not want his or her breast or fanny touched.

I don't know. I think some really cool things have been taken away. And this is from a straight man who was once photographed with his hand up under the blouse of a female co-worker.

And I'd do it again under the same circumstances. She needed help, she asked for my help, and I helped her in a "gentlemanly" way. Sure, I'd do it again.

And the boss would probably call me in again for a lecture on how to treat female co-workers. But then, he didn't get a chance to hear the conversation before and after what certainly appeared to be an apparent "grope."

Chapter Thirteen

Let's take one more look at the by-now famous double page spread in the Los Angeles Times focusing on the entertainment business and what this spread really says. This is different than the single page spread with the unrecognizable caricature of, I'm guessing, Hugh Hefner of Playboy fame. This spread in the Times names names. The two page spread also names names, but the one page ad called "Twilight of the Creeps" and drawn by "Horsey" is the one with Hefner. Both, all three pages, the double page and the single page, are beneath the dignity of a newspaper like the L.A. Times.

Do you know "Louis C.K." in the double page spread? He has for years, according to the Times, denied *"rumors"* of "inappropriate behavior." But then five women *"alleged incidents"* of him masturbating, or requesting to do so, in front of them. He admitted to some of these acts, and has faded from sight. His deals with HBO, Netflix and FX are on hold. Hang in there Louis, it isn't over yet.

Then there was the short piece on John Conyers on the double page, with a rather unflattering drawing of John, a member of the House of Representatives, who has denied any wrongdoing amid *accusations* of sexual harassment by female employees. His support from House minority leader Nancy Pelosi and others has collapsed.

And what about famed newsman and "Today" co-anchor Matt Lauer, *accused* of "inappropriate sexual behavior in a workplace." Lauer went so far as to say, "Some of what is being said about me is untrue or mischaracterized, but there is enough truth…to make me feel embarrassed and ashamed."

Until a number of women *alleged* sexual misconduct against him, including a charge that he sexually assaulted a sixteen year old girl when he was in his thirties, Roy Moore, former Alabama Supreme Court chief justice was a sure thing to win a Senate seat. Moore has denied the allegations.

Charlie Rose, a host on "CBS This Morning" and a "Sixty Minutes" correspondent, was fired by CBS after several women *accused* him of sexual misconduct. Rose apologized and said, "I have behaved insensitively at times, and I accept responsibility for that, though I do not believe that all of these *allegations* are accurate."

Have you noticed the "alleged" and "accused" and "rumors" and other soft words? And let's make one other thing very crystal clear. This study is in no way meant to excuse real sexual harassment, which has obviously happened, and continues to happen. But a blanket "you're guilty as sin" in every case is not right or proper in the United States of America.

We will probe a little deeper into the Los Angeles Times double page spread entitled "At First a Whisper, and Then a Roar." Next in line is chef Mario Batali, who was reported to have been fired from "The Chew" after a website, "Eater," said that four women accused the chef of touching them inappropriately, although their identity was not revealed. There is that word "*accused*" again, although Batali did say, according to the Times, that the behavior in the report does "match up with ways I have acted."

And what about Assemblyman Raul Bocanegra, who became the first California lawmaker to resign over sexual harassment allegations throughout his career? Both Bocanegra and Assemblyman Matt Dababneh, who also said he is resigning for the same reason, say that "a legislative inquiry will clear their names."

Senator Al Franken, who said he will resign soon after several women accused him of sexual misconduct, which included "forcing them to kiss him," agreed that such charges should be heard, but that he had given a "false impression" that he was admitting guilt.

John Lasseter, who is the chief creative officer of Pixar and takes credit for the new hit animated film "Coco," has taken a leave of absence after apologizing to those people who have received "an unwanted hug or any other gesture."

Bill O'Reilly, a former Fox News host, was fired amid sexual harassment *allegations*. It is possible that he or the network also paid off some women who alleged sexual harassment or *verbal abuse*. Once the networks top-rated personality, he has denied all allegations.

Warner Bros. is said to have decided to cancel a deal with filmmaker and producer/director Brett Ratner and his company, RatPac-Dune Entertainment, after he was *accused* by several women of sexual misconduct or harassment. Ratner denies the allegations.

Actor Kevin Spacey may have figured a way around *accusations*. Accused of unwanted sexual advances by another male actor, Spacey simply said "I choose now to live as a gay man." He was dropped from "House of Cards" and replaced in "All the Money in the World."

And perhaps Jeffrey Tambor also has the right idea. Two women accused him while on the set of "Transparent," and he said, "The idea that I would deliberately harass anyone is simply and utterly untrue." And he is not returning to the show due to the "politicized atmosphere."

Russell Simmons founded Def Jam Recordings, and has now been accused by several women of different sexual misconduct acts. He has apologized, but also denied all allegations of misconduct.

Charlie Rose, the former host of "CBS This Morning" and a "60 Minutes" correspondent, was fired after several women *accused* him of sexual misconduct. Rose did apologize, and said, "I have behaved insensitively at times, and I accept responsibility for that, though I do not believe that all of these allegations are accurate."

James Toback was accused by thirty eight women of sexual misconduct. He is a well known director of films, and says he has never met any of the women. If he did meet any of them, it was "for five minutes and I have no recollection." The list has now grown to more than three hundred women, according to the Times. Toback denies all allegations.

Finally, on the double page spread in the Los Angeles Times on December 31, 2017, is the caricature of Harvey Weinstein, who has been *accused* of sexual misbehavior all the way to rape by more than eighty women. He was quickly fired by the company he owns and kicked out of the motion picture academy. He is at this time the focus of several criminal investigations and lawsuits, and at the moment still categorically denies any crimes.

There is little doubt that some of these women "came on" to men like Harvey Weinstein and any number of others. Only Linda Lovelace had the skill, and control of her "choking mechanism" to accomplish what she was able to do to men. But Weinstein was famous, and powerful, and had a position of importance in Hollywood. He could, with a wave of his hand, arrange for an excellent role for any actress. There are rumors about how Marilyn Monroe came on to President Kennedy and other men in show business, but they are just rumors. According to her, she didn't, but according to Brigitte Bardot, she probably did. Revealing that information is up to Marilyn Monroe and Marilyn, sadly, if now gone.

There is no answer to this rash of accusations and lawsuits. Many will be settled by the payment of money, some will be settled by admission of guilt and a request for forgiveness. A few will be battled out in courtrooms in Hollywood and around the United States, where women will finally be heard.

Some celebrities may go to jail, where they belong.

Some women may go to jail, for making false accusations against very powerful men.

All the author of this book is reasonably certain of is that actresses Gwyneth Paltrow, Angelina Jolie and Heather Graham have all made claims against Mr. Weinstein. This much was online, and might or might not be accurate, as online things often are, or are not.

And also at the last ceremony where actors pat themselves on the back and get small trophies for a good acting job, some in the audience were shouting about "changing their vote" when they heard about one of their favorites admitting he was gay.

All he did was to agree that he is gay, for God's sake. He didn't confess to murder, or rape, or anything else illegal. All he said was "I choose to live my life as a gay man."

Why can't we just choose to allow him to do so?

Maybe we should all just slow down, as actor Liam Neeson suggested, and think things over. Most men know it is not a crime to just "play around" hoping to maybe "get lucky." Sometimes we did get lucky, but more often we did not. Those days seem to be gone forever, and that is too bad. But playing around is not a crime, rape is a crime and should result in a long term in prison.

Many women are now saying they have been raped. This may be true, assuming they didn't "play around" ahead of time and even opened the door to rape. Some men are dumb, even rich men who have been "babied" all their life where the opposite sex is concerned. Some men, especially rich men, think they *deserve* sex just because they are rich. They may be ugly as sin, but, hey, a little sex will feel good. So they take what they think they deserve, or what they think is being offered, or offer what they have to trade, and "no big deal."

Rape is a big deal, a crime, and being rich doesn't make it less a crime. Any enforced sex is a crime. For that matter, slapping someone on the back, offered as a sign of friendship, is also a crime, and from now on will apparently be a crime.

You have shown great intelligence by struggling through this book.

You figure it out and make your own judgments while the courts struggle to do the same.